ThinkingJewellery
// Two

arnoldsche Art Publishers

ThinkingJewellery

// Two

Wilhelm Lindemann / Theo Smeets (eds.)

Trier University of Applied Sciences,
Campus for Gemstones and Jewellery, Idar-Oberstein
in cooperation with Jakob Bengel Foundation, Idar-Oberstein

arnoldsche Art Publishers

Preface

„May your lecture not be directly related to jewellery."

With this sentence we invite the speakers of the symposium ThinkingJewellery to give a lecture. Critical voices said: „and when are we going to make jewellery?", thus masking the fact that the attempt at a transfer between science and art is probably very exhausting. We have already held our symposium eleven times. This publication is a follow-up to the book „SchmuckDenken" published in 2011, in which we collected lectures from the first six editions, and at the same time it is a prelude to something new. Since the symposium will now take place bi-annually, the Campus Idar-Oberstein in cooperation with the Jakob Bengel-Stiftung and the city of Idar-Oberstein will publish a series of publications in the „interim years" that will collect and expand part of the contributions to SchmuckDenken.

I wish you lots of joy and new insights with ThinkingJewellery 2!

Theo Smeets
Head of Department Gemstones and Jewellery

Contents

Olaf Müller

A Brief History of Polarity in Physics[1]

Introduction

During the second half of the eighteenth century, the conception of polarity spread rapidly among scientists in diverse fields. Though it proved fruitful, it has since fallen into obscurity.[2] To date there is no accurate account of how the conception of polarity emerged, how it should be understood and why it is valuable. I will address this lacuna by introducing some highlights from polarity in the history of physics. My aim is to give a rational reconstruction of some ideas which appear outdated but are interesting enough to warrant reconsideration. I'll challenge some established views of current physics in the spirit of what Hasok Chang calls complementary science.[3]

To preempt a potential misunderstanding, I am not interested in the history of the word 'polarity' and its transliterations in other languages – after all one can express thoughts involving polarity without knowing any technical term. Rather I am interested in thoughts of a certain form which may but need not be expressed with the word. A theorist who describes polar structures without

1 This essay is based on my talk 'Goethe on Colours – a Vindication', given on 14 October 2017 at the conference 'ThinkingJewellery XI', Trier University of Applied Sciences, Campus Idar-Oberstein. I would like to thank the audience for interesting questions and constructive criticism. Many thanks to Emanuel Viebahn and Troy Vine for valuable support with the translation of the written version.

2 Nevertheless even modern physics shows traces of the idea of polarity (e.g., in the symmetry between particles and anti-particles; Henley et al. 2007, pp. 108–12).

3 See (as applied to the history of chemistry) Chang 2013.

labelling them 'polar' can still implicitly have the concept of polarity at their disposal.

The conception of polarity can operate at different levels of generality. A local use of the conception may help capture certain symmetrical structures in a particular field of investigation – for example, magnetism; this is where my account of polarity will get off the ground. At the other end of the scale, the conception of polarity can be used with *unrestrained generality*. Such uses cover the most diverse fields and are often conjoined with the claim that nature as a whole is constituted by polar structures.[4] According to this claim a comprehensive network of polarities connects every occurrence with every other. I can only briefly touch on this bold idea here, which obviously can hardly be propounded without using technical terms such as 'polar' and its derivatives.

Amber and magnets

The concept of polarity probably emerged in early observations of magnetism; Petrus Peregrinus spoke of a magnet having two poles as early as the thirteenth century.[5] Although at that time there was no abstract expression (e.g., 'polarity') for the structural characteristics of magnets, such structures came to light with sufficient clarity; here we can assume an implicit use of polarity.[6]

Here is a case that exemplifies the structures at issue: the red end of a bar magnet attracts the green end of another bar magnet; if we rotate one of the two magnets such that their green ends face each another, the opposite happens – they repel. In short: reversing the spatial orientation of a magnet and thus reversing its poles causes an *inversion* of the forces.

From the very beginning of systematic research into magnetism, scientists suspected that electrostatic phenomena were another case of magnetism. This conjecture was repudiated by William Gilbert, who demonstrated that the forces of attraction of electrostatically charged amber are not magnetic forces.[7] Still it remained a popular view that electricity must be governed by the same (or at least analogous)

---

4 See e.g. Schelling 1857, p. 476.

5 See Steinle 2012, pp. 109–10 with references to the original literature.

6 To my knowledge there is no account of when words such as 'polarity' were first used in the sense at issue here.

7 Gilbert 1893, pp. 74–98; Gilbert 1600, pp. 47–61 (= Liber II, Cap. II–III).

laws as magnetism – that is, by polar laws. What exactly does that mean? Polarity in the relevant sense is meant to apply to two regions or elements of an experimental setup, the two poles, which create a specific kind of symmetry. The structure of this symmetry is such that interchanging the two poles reverses a particular effect, leaving everything else unchanged. Does the phenomenon of electricity display this symmetry too? It does, but it took a long time before it was empirically verified, as I will show in the next section.

Aepin and the tourmaline

For two years from 1755, Franz Ulrich Theodosius Aepin was director of the Berlin Observatory. Although he was employed as an astronomer, he researched a wide field of topics within physics and mathematics. Aepin was convinced of the simplicity of nature and applied this principle to electricity and magnetism: '*Among those who are familiar with this habit of nature, there have been scholars who thought that magnetic and electrical forces, these wonders of nature little known to the ancients, have the same or similar origins. And it has to be said that these scholars deserve applause rather than apology. For while it must be admitted that those who had the idea of the similarity of these two forces have so far expressed conjectures rather than knowledge, we should not blame them for showing us the proper path towards knowledge of nature.*'[8]

Aepin faced great difficulties in bringing electricity and magnetism under uniform laws, until a coincidence played into his hands: '*Many years ago I had similar thoughts and searched for the path to these secrets of nature. But the path was so arduous that I became tired and could not pursue the investigations any further. However, recently nature became more inclined to me and encouraged me to go on. A certain stone fell into my hands which is not only endowed with electrical powers but also shines with other wonderful qualities; I deemed it worthy of further observation as it seemed to have powers that were very similar to those of magnets.*'[9]

Aepin was referring to tourmaline [fig. 2], a beautiful gemstone that had recently arrived from Ceylon and Brazil. When heated, the stone attracted fine ash particles and could thus be used to clean tobacco pipes – a miracle of electrical powers, as it turned out.

---

8 Aepin 1760, pp. 4–5; footnote omitted, our translation.

9 Ibid., pp. 5–6, our translation.

It had been known for some time that there are two kinds of electricity, which were described as positive and negative.[10] Aepin's experiments with his tourmaline provided the first good reason to speak of negative and positive poles of electricity – in analogy to the north and south poles of the magnet: '*One side of the heated tourmaline is always electrically positive, the other always negative. It thus has both kinds of electricity at the same time, like the magnet has twofold magnetism. Furthermore it is not only similar to the magnet in that it has two poles: in both repelling and attracting, it also observes rules that are identical to those governing the behaviour of magnets.*'[11]

Aepin seized the opportunity and immediately tried to generalise the discovery he had made with tourmaline. His attempts were successful: he managed to create pairs of positive and negative poles on many other objects.[12]

It might seem surprising that the structural analogy between magnetism and electricity had not been noticed before. This may have to do with the fact that the two kinds of electricity had not often been observed on one and the same body. Aepin had learned from Benjamin Franklin's writings that both kinds of electricity are present on a charged Leyden jar (an early capacitor).[13] But in this case, one kind of electricity is on the inside of the jar, while its counterpart is on the outside. Thus the geometrical situation differs from that of the magnet: inside and outside fit less to the idea of two poles than opposite sides of an object. In short: the tourmaline was needed to show the analogy between electricity and magnetism.

Kant's negative magnitudes

Shortly after his groundbreaking research on the electrical properties of tourmaline, Aepin was appointed to a chair in St. Petersburg. The journey there would normally have taken him via Königsberg, and so he may well have met Immanuel Kant. Regardless of whether the two scholars did meet on this occasion, Kant swiftly reacted to Aepin's results and generalised his research method. In 1763 he published a small booklet with the following title: *Versuch den Begriff*

10 Ibid., pp. 9–13. Also see Steinle 2013, pp. 54–60.

11 Aepin 1760, pp. 16–7, our translation; cf. ibid., p. 32.

12 Ibid., pp. 20–1, esp. second footnote.

13 Ibid., p. 20, first footnote.

der negativen Größen in die Weltweisheit einzuführen (Attempt to Introduce the Concept of Negative Magnitudes into Philosophy).[14] Kant had recognised the potential of the idea of confronting a given magnitude with its negative counterpart. In his view this move always requires the same conceptual procedure, regardless of the area to which it is applied.[15] As Kant wanted to show the analogous role of pairs of opposites in diverse areas, he took great pains to explicate the conception of negative magnitudes.[16] In particular he contrasted cases of polarity with cases where we find only one factor in play; in the latter cases we do not posit a second, contrary factor but rather speak of the presence or absence of the one factor.

We are acquainted with both kinds of cases. For magnetism and electricity, not only the north or plus pole is taken to be effective but also the south or minus pole. Such cases of true polarity involve what Kant calls real opposition and will be my focus here.[17] There are also cases in physics where the idea of polarity is not evoked, such as thermodynamics and optics. While in everyday discourse we speak of heat and coldness or of brightness and darkness, their apparent polarity goes against well-established physical theories: coldness does not really exist; it is nothing more than the absence of heat – similarly darkness is nothing more than the absence of light.

In Kant's time it was far from clear which areas of physics were governed by polarities – that is, by real oppositions. Concerning heat Kant wrote: '*There is, for example, the well-known question whether coolness requires a positive cause, or whether as a lack it is to be attributed simply to the absence of the cause of heat. I should like to consider this matter a little, at least as far as it is relevant*

14 Kant 2002; for the German original see Kant 1912. The reference to Aepin is to be found in Kant 2002, p. 224/Kant 1912, p. 185.

15 According to Adickes this 'drive to synopsis and synthesis' is distinctive of Kant's general way of thinking (Adickes 1924, pp. 51, 53, 308 et passim).

16 Kant 2002, Section I/Kant 1912, first section.

17 Kant used several different expressions to describe the same relation: 'Realrepugnanz' (real repugnancy), 'Realopposition' (real opposition), 'reale Entgegensetzung' or 'wirkliche Entgegensetzung' (real or actual juxtaposition), 'Realentgegensetzung' (real juxtaposition); see Kant 1912, pp. 172, 174–7; compare the slightly different translations in Kant 2002, pp. 212, 214, 215, 217. He had the *concept* of polarity but not the *word*. Of course the word itself is unimportant, and the variety of expressions Kant uses is less a sign of conceptual unclarity than of his inability to coin a catchy expression. At the same time his vocabulary has the advantage of being sufficiently remote from magnetism, making it better suited than 'polarity' for universal application.

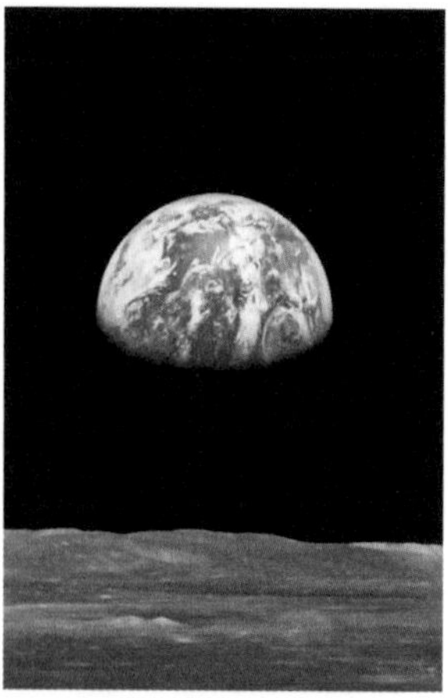

fig. 1

The earth seen from the moon.
The beauty of the earth's colours competes with that of tourmaline. Furthermore both the earth and tourmaline can be characterised with the help of poles. The earth has two magnetic poles; a charged tourmaline has two electrical poles.
Photo: NASA

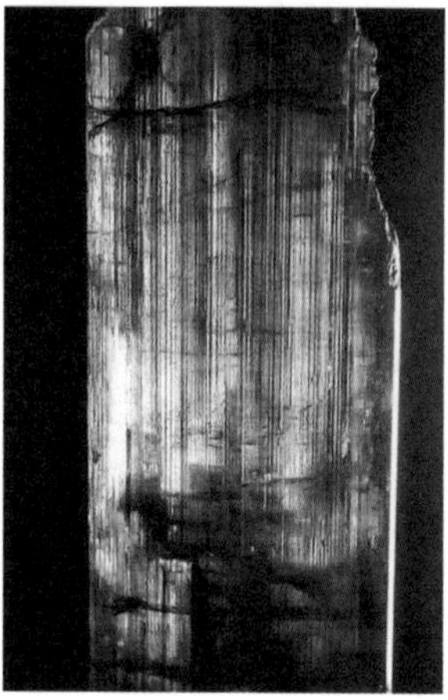

fig. 2

Tourmaline.
Tourmalines can be found in many different colours. We have chosen a stone that shows colours similar to those of our planet. If a tourmaline is heated, a positive electrical pole forms at one end and a negative pole at the other.
Photo: Géry Parent

to my purposes. Doubtless, coldness itself is simply the negation of warmth, and it can easily be seen that it is possible in itself, even in the absence of any positive cause. But it can with equal ease be seen that it can also be the effect of a positive cause, and that it does actually on occasion arise from such a cause – and all this can be understood independently of what opinion one may entertain concerning the origin of warmth. Absolute coldness is unknown in nature, and if it is discussed, then it is understood only in a comparative sense.' [18]

After reporting on Aepin's results, Kant boldly transferred them to the current case: *'Now, my contention is this: whenever the temperature is raised or lowered, in other words, whenever the degree of heat or coldness is changed, and in particular changed rapidly, and whenever that change occurs at one end of a continuous intervening space, or at one end of an elongated body what happens is this. There are always two poles, so to speak, of warmth to be found: one of them is positive, that is to say, its temperature is higher than the previous temperature of the body in question, while the other pole is negative, its temperature, namely, being lower than the previous temperature of the body; in other words, it is cold.'*[19]

Kant supported his claim with experiments and observations which in his eyes bolstered the analogy between magnetic or electrical poles on the one hand and poles of heat versus coldness on the other; furthermore he speculated about experiments that were yet to be carried out and would (he hoped) support his claim.[20]

The earth, a giant tourmaline? fig. 1, fig. 2

The boldest (and perhaps most dubious) thought Kant expressed in his work on negative magnitudes was the idea that coldness exists in itself. Surprisingly this thought was soon developed further in research on tourmalines. Kant had known of the initial stages of this research but had gone far beyond it in his speculations. In 1766

18 Kant 2002, p. 223, endnote omitted/Kant 1912, p. 184.

19 Kant 2002, p. 224/Kant 1912, p. 186.

20 Kant 2002, pp. 225–6/Kant 1912, pp. 186–7 (esp. footnote). At first sight the experimental results Kant counted upon appear implausible; according to Adickes the most important experiment Kant mentioned was bound to fail (Adickes 1924, p. 7 with reference to Kant 2002, pp. 225–6n/Kant 1912, pp. 186–7n). However, Lord Rumford shortly afterwards conducted further experiments which fit Kant's general thesis of a real opposition between heat and coldness surprisingly well (Chang 2002).

Swedish chemist Torbern Bergman published a two-volume monograph describing and expanding the very latest insights about our planet: *Physick Beskrifning Ofver Jordklotet* (Physical Description of the Earth).[21]

In a chapter about lightning and similar phenomena (such as ball lightning), Bergman took up the idea of coldness as a force in itself, radicalising it and connecting it to electrical polarity. This culminated in the following speculation: *'Might coldness generate positive electricity and heat negative electricity? Might the force of the antipodes be opposed to the force we can detect? In a tourmaline both kinds of force can only be generated by changing the temperature in the surrounding medium [...]. Perhaps certain mountains and places on the globe are of the same nature as a tourmaline.'*[22]

This thought may have been based on the idea that the coldness at the magnetic north pole of the earth is related to the generation of certain forms of electricity; if this were indeed the case, then different climate zones should correlate with specific electricity distributions. Such considerations were advanced by physicist Georg Christoph Lichtenberg in 1778: *'Might not the globe be a giant tourmaline whose poles roughly coincide with those of the earth: the positive pole with the north pole and the negative pole with the south pole? As this may seem too bold to some, I want to explicate my notion of this tourmaline. I do not take it to be a gemstone of enormous size hidden under the surface of the earth. Rather I take it to be the sum of all objects scattered across the earth, including the air, which is electrified by the heat of the earth or the sun and which can transmit its electricity to all objects.'*[23]

Note that Lichtenberg wasn't a romantic enthusiast but the first German professor of experimental physics and firmly rooted in the tradition of the Enlightenment. He used the idea of the earth as a giant tourmaline for far-reaching theoretical aims.[24] As an accomplished writer he must have been aware of the suggestive power

---

21 Bergman 1773, Bergman 1774. For the German version see Bergman 1780a, 1780b.

22 Bergman 1780b, p. 65, our translation.

23 Lichtenberg 1956, p. 44, our translation.

24 This was first pointed out by Wiesenfeldt and Breidbach, who also connected Lichtenberg's formulations with earlier work on tourmalines and who suggested that the Enlightenment's concept of polarity as applied to tourmalines is closely related to the concept of polarity in romantic physics and Naturphilosophie (Wiesenfeldt and Breidbach 2012).

of the picture he had drawn. Given photographs of our blue planet, Lichtenberg's picture seems surprisingly fitting. Doesn't the earth really look like a tourmaline?

To summarise, we have seen how scientists and scientifically minded philosophers expanded the concept of polarity to ever new fields of investigation: starting from magnetism the concept was transferred to electricity and then to the opposition of coldness and heat, which was finally connected with other polar phenomena. All this was normal science, neither amateurish nor esoteric. On the contrary it was advanced research carried out by leading scientists of the time.

They actively sought out phenomena that could be systematised with the help of polar structures. In Kant's terminology the concept of polarity functioned as a 'regulative idea' – that is, as a guiding principle for research.[25] From today's perspective the strategy was successful in some cases and unsuccessful in others. But the current perspective doesn't always give an accurate idea of how researchers reasoned in earlier times. It is helpful to bear in mind that around 1800 the search for polarities was a successful research programme that had many adherents.

How Newton drove polarity out of optics

Before Newton revolutionised optics with the publication of his prismatic experiments in 1672 [fig. 3], it was thought that colours emerged from the interplay of light and darkness.[26] The pre-Newtonian theories of colour differ in detail, but they all entail a symmetrical opposition of light and darkness. Newton denounced this consensus by conceptualising darkness as the absence of light rather than an active factor in its own right.[27]

According to his conception of optics, only rays of light are optically effective. He not only defended this claim on a theoretical level but also presupposed it in his empirical work. That Newton's

25 See in particular Kant 1976 A, pp. 642–68 and B, pp. 670–96. Kant was not explicitly concerned with the regulative idea of polarity but rather with that of homogeneity (for further discussion of this topic, see Müller 2013a, Sections 2.5 and 3). While Kant did not use the notion of a regulative idea in his pre-critical writings, he came close to it on several occasions, in particular when discussing polarity (Kant 2002, pp. 225–6n/Kant 1912, pp. 186–7n). This may have been an echo of a similar thought by Aepin (1760, p. 5, see above, last sentence of the first quote on section III).

26 On this and the following, see e.g. Zemplén 2001, Nakajima 1984.

27 Newton 1671/2, p. 3085 et passim.

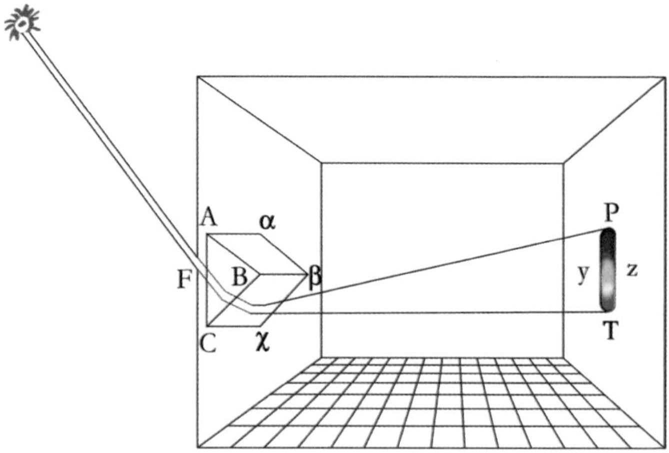

fig. 3

Newton's decomposition of sunlight (1672).
A ray of sunlight shines through the hole in the window shutter F onto a prism, where it is refracted and decomposed into its coloured components.

Illustration by Matthias Herder and Ingo Nussbaumer following a black and white drawing from Newton's lecture notes, see ill. 2 in Newton 1973, p. 3 experiments are based on a monistic conception of optics is reflected by the fact that they are conducted in dark surroundings, in the famous camera obscura. Indeed some of his experiments only work in this setting. With respect to one of the most difficult experiments, he wrote, '*[…] 'tis requisite that the Room be made very dark, least any scattering light, mixing with the colour, disturb and allay it.*'[28]

Newton was convinced that darkness is required to minimise disturbing factors and produce clear results. It is easy to see that this approach leaves no room for darkness as an independent causal factor; Newton used darkness as a neutral background for optical experimentation.

It took several decades for the new theory to assert itself.[29] But once Newton's *Opticks* (1704) had spread across Europe, views giving darkness an independent causal role disappeared. When Goethe entered the debate a century later and suggested returning to a polar conception of optics, he certainly went against the prevailing orthodoxy. This does not mean, however, that his approach was unheard of or unscientific.[30] Goethe had witnessed how new ideas quickly became established in fields such as chemistry, and he knew of the successful polar research programme outlined above. Against this background Goethe's systematic search for polarities in the realm of colours was far from outlandish.

Goethe's polar research programme in optics

Goethe made clear that he wanted to transfer the terminology of polarity from fields such as magnetism and electricity to optics: '*Scientists have obviously felt that it would be necessary and suitable to use a figurative language […], for the formula of polarity has been borrowed from magnetism and extended to electricity, etc. The concepts of plus and minus, which represent this formula, have found suitable application to many a phenomenon […]. We, too, have long wished to introduce the term polarity into the theory of color, and the present work will show our justification and purpose in doing so.*'[31]

---

28 Ibid., p. 3087, italics mine.

29 Shapiro 1996.

30 Pace Duck 2016, pp. xxii, xxviii et passim; more on this topic in Müller 2018b, Sections 1–2.

31 Goethe 1988, §§756–7. Similar remarks are to be found in ibid., §453 and pp. 158–9. The latter passage merely implicitly describes the polar strategy through a host of examples but does not feature the corresponding expression; it is discussed in detail in Müller 2018a, Section 5.

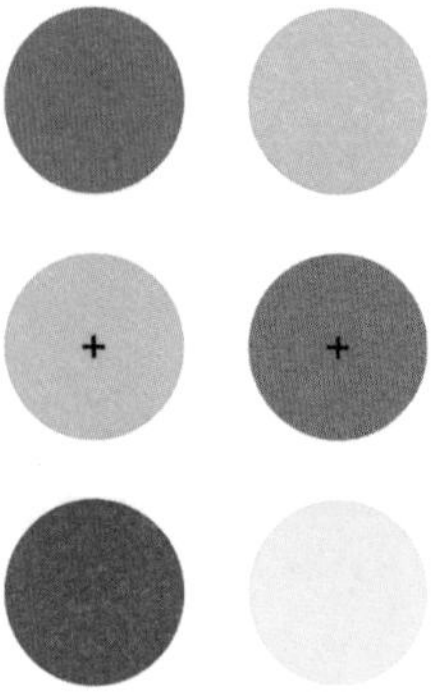

fig. 4

Complementary colours.
Three colours from Newton's prismatic experiments (red, green, blue) are placed beside their complements (turquoise, magenta, yellow). To elicit coloured afterimages, cover one of the two rows with white paper and stare at the black cross for about ten seconds. Then look at the white paper without moving your eyes.
Illustration by Sarah Schalk and Olaf Müller

fig. 5

Template to generate Newton's spectrum.
In a well-lit environment, place a glass prism on the template with its three edges parallel to the bottom of the page. Look at the white dot through the prism, slowly moving the prism towards your eye. Its upper and lower edges gradually become coloured. If you rotate the prism about its axis at the right distance, you'll see Newton's spectrum of red/yellow/green/turquoise/blue fig. 3. If the distance is varied, different stages of Newton's spectrum (with fewer colours) will be seen.
Illustration by Benjamin Marschall

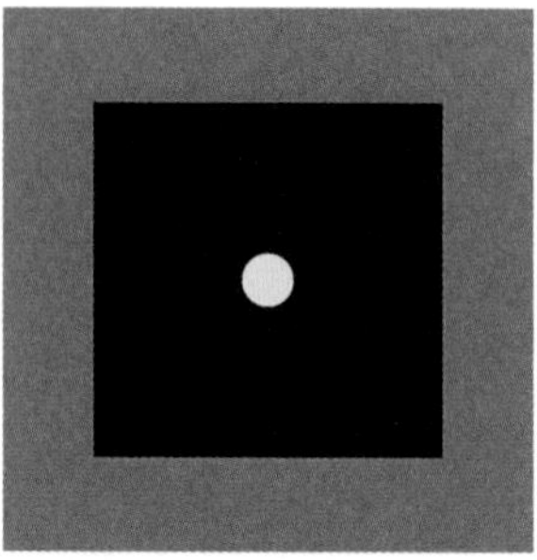

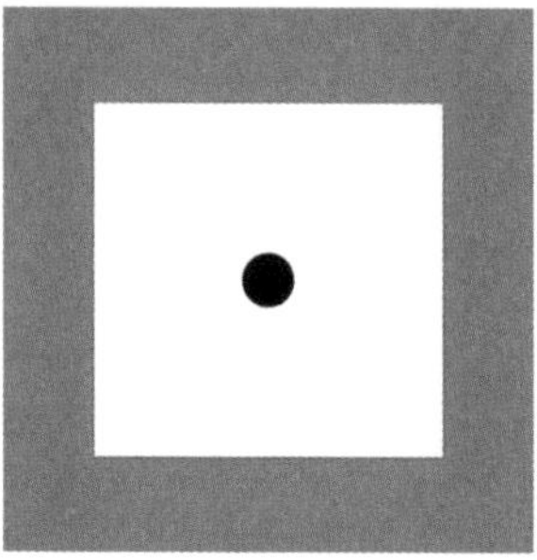

fig. 6

Inverted template to generate Goethe's spectrum.
Goethe's spectrum can be generated in the same way as Newton's, using an inversion of the previous template.
Illustration by Benjamin Marschall

Interpreters have not taken this programmatic statement seriously, perhaps because they have not associated it with those experiments that show how it is to be understood.[32] It might therefore be helpful to present some of the optical experiments in which Goethe employed polarity as a guiding principle.

He managed to show [fig. 4] that each colour has a polar opposite, its complementary colour, shown by the colour's afterimage.[33] This phenomenon is nowadays known as successive contrast. Complementary colours feature not only in physiological experiments but also in physics. If, for example, one looks through a prism at a white circle in black surroundings [fig. 5], the resulting spectrum [fig. 7] can be transformed into its complement [fig. 8] by inverting the contrast – that is, by looking at a black circle in white surroundings [fig. 6]. In Goethe's words: '*I had fixed a white disc onto a black background. If viewed through a prism from a certain distance, the disc led to the familiar spectrum and thus replicated Newton's main experiment in his camera obscura. However, a black disc on a white background also created a colourful and indeed more splendid spectre.*'[34]

Goethe systematised these so-called subjective experiments, which were already known in his time [fig. 10]. Furthermore he was the first to display their polarity on a screen in a so-called objective experiment.[35] Whereas Newton sent a narrow ray of light through a darkened prism and captured its decomposition into blue/ turquoise/green/ yellow/red on a screen [fig. 3 and 9 left], Goethe directed a narrow shadow through an illuminated prism and captured the complementary spectrum of the colours yellow/red/magenta/blue/ turquoise [fig. 9 right].[36]

In those days it was a challenge to show this effect in sufficient clarity. Small glass prisms were not suited for the purpose, so Goethe had a large water prism made [fig. 11] and proudly recounted his eventual success: '*My aim was to repeat all the results of the subjective*

---

32 See e.g. Böhler 2018, Section 3, Eckle 2015, p. 235, Kötter 2017, p. 157.

33 See Goethe 1988, §§47–60.

34 Goethe 1957a, p. 420, our translation. Goethe used the German expression for ghost (*Gespenst*) to play on the ambiguity of 'spectre'.

35 It is easy to see why Goethe calls the former experiments subjective and the latter ones objective (see next quotation). Newton also relied on subjective experiments but without that name; for instance, the first experiment in his *Opticks* is a subjective experiment (Newton 1964, pp. 17–8).

36 On the subjective or objective production of these experiments, see Goethe 1988, §§215, 331.

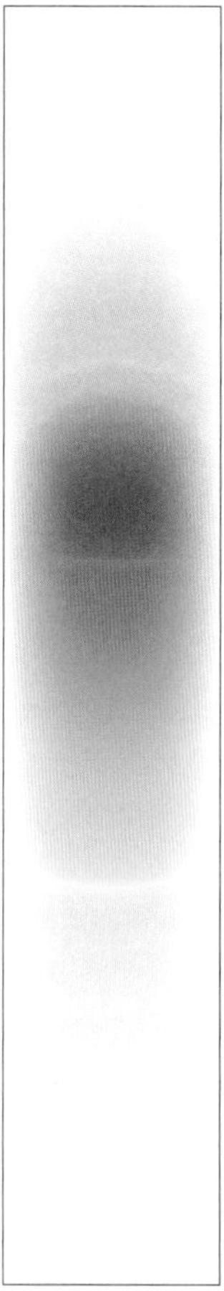

fig. 7

Newton's spectrum.
Result of observing fig. 5 through a prism. Both order and orientation of the colours red/yellow/green/turquoise/blue depend on the orientation of the prism.
Illustration by Olaf Müller

fig. 8

Inversion of Newton's spectrum.
Result of observing fig. 6 through a prism; fig. 7 and 8 are related via a symmetry operation (similar to the example of magnetism, p. 10). If the poles of light and darkness in the experimental set up of fig. 5 and 6 are exchanged, the visible colours will be inverted.
Illustration by Olaf Müller

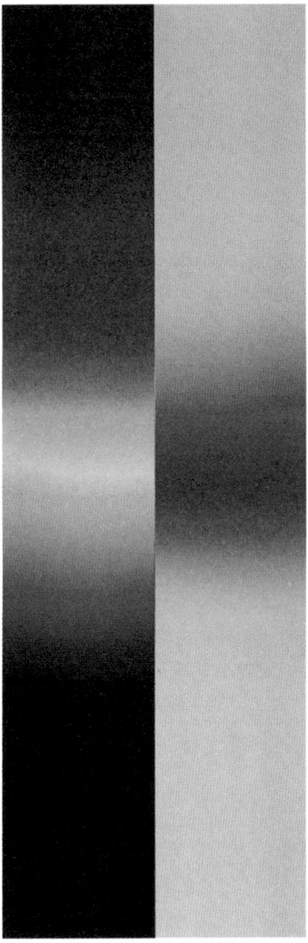

fig. 9

Newton's and Goethe's spectrum compared.

Each colour in one spectrum is adjacent to its complement in the other. The spectra shown here appear more orderly than those in fig. 7 and 8, as they have been created using a rectangular light source instead of a circular one.

Illustration by Ingo Nussbaumer, edited by Matthias Herder experiments [that is, those viewed through the prism] in objective experiments [with the spectra captured on a screen]. The small size of prisms was a problem. I had a larger prism made [...] and placed cardboard apertures next to it in order to create all the effects that a view through a prism had made visible on my templates.'[37]

'Objective experiments often use the luminous form of the sun, but seldom a dark form. We have found a convenient way to arrange such an experiment. Let us place our large water prism in the sunlight and glue a round cardboard disc to its outer or inner face.'[38]

Goethe had presented an optical experiment par excellence: exact, objective, replicable and no less physical than its Newtonian predecessor. The size of the prism meant that the experiment required considerable technical effort. Goethe didn't shy away from such efforts and experimented in a laboratory that was more suitable than Newton's.[39]

Not content with one pair of complementary spectra [fig. 9], Goethe varied the distance between prism and screen.[40] It turned out that such variation changed not only the size of Newton's spectrum but also its colours – and exactly the same was the case with Goethe's complementary spectrum and its colours.[41] Goethe had to take precise measurements to demonstrate this. He presented the twofold series of experiments in a pair of carefully drawn and coloured illustrations [figs. 12 and 13].

Where Goethe's research programme was held up and how it should carry on

To sum up my account of Goethe's research in optics, he managed to demonstrate experimentally the polarity between light and darkness as well as between complementary colours. How does the polarity of light and darkness relate to the polarities in electricity and magnetism? In all three of these fields, exchanging two poles leads to an inversion of certain effects: in electricity and magnetism, forces are inverted, in optics, colours. Goethe's polarity in optics is thus structurally analogous to established theories in other fields.

---

37 Goethe 1957a, p. 422, our translation.

38 Goethe 1988, §331.

39 For many helpful details on this point, see Klinger and Müller 2008.

40 See Goethe 1988, §§324–31.

41 Ibid., §§204–17 on the subjective spectra and Goethe, and §§317–34 on the objective spectra.

Goethe knew that the experimental support for Newton's theory was not confined to the small number of experiments I have mentioned so far.[42] In propagating his polar research agenda in optics, Goethe had to claim that other experiments of Newton's also have polar opposites, namely all of the replicable experiments in the *Opticks* on which Newton based his theory. This claim I'll call 'Goethe's theorem'.[43] Though he was unable to invert all of Newton's experiments, this was due to the experimental limitations of his time and not due to the theorem itself. For in order to systematically exchange light and darkness in these experiments, Newton's dark chamber has to be inverted (by constructing a light chamber which is uniformly illuminated). That was impossible for Goethe, as the electric light was not invented until some decades after his death.

How does Goethe's theorem fare from today's point of view, now that it is possible to construct such light chambers? Surprisingly Goethe's theorem holds up both experimentally and theoretically.[44] Indeed Newton's most important experiments have been successfully inverted. For example, in Newton's white synthesis the colours of his spectrum are recombined to create white; if the colours of Goethe's spectrum are recombined in the same manner, darkness results.[45] And whereas in the *experimentum crucis* an isolated spectral colour does not decompose when projected through a second prism, in its inversion an isolated colour from Goethe's spectrum does not decompose either when projected through a second prism in light surroundings.[46]

---

42 Goethe 2016.

43 See Müller 2018a, Section 3. Goethe's theorem not only concerns those experiments Newton described but must include all experiments that can be conducted in what is now known as geometrical optics (Müller 2015, §II.5.22). Neither Newton nor Goethe had a clear conception of this modern discipline, but including its experiments in the theorem is natural from a systematic point of view.

44 Bjerke was the first to carry out research in this vein (Bjerke 1963, pp. 32, 65–6, 85–8 et passim).

45 As demonstrated e.g. by Nussbaumer 2008, pp. 105, 158, 188. See fig. 18, images 1 and 2 as well as Müller 2016, Section 6 and Müller 2010, Sections VII (white synthesis) and XV (black synthesis).

46 The idea of this inversion is due to Goethe, although he was unable to realise it empirically (Goethe 2016, §132). For early theoretical advances, see Holtsmark 1970. The first empirical results were achieved by Sällström 2010. See Müller 2016, p. 339, n. 23 for a brief summary (in English) as well as Rang and Müller 2009 for more details (in German). The fullest account is given in Rang 2015.

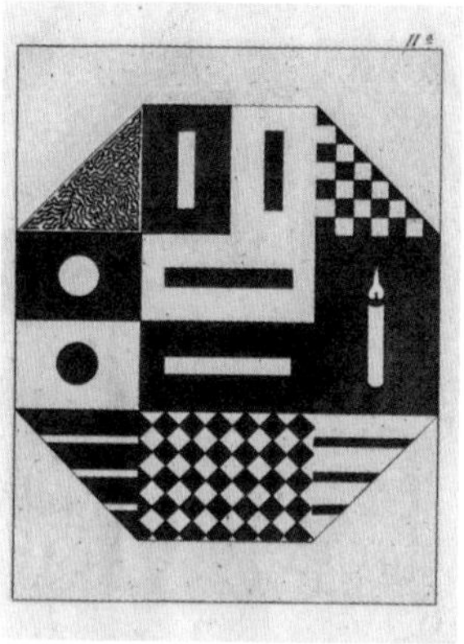

fig. 10

Goethe's template for prismatic experiments.
In many of Goethe's experiments, a template is observed through a prism. He designed these templates to ensure that the relevant optical situation is reversed.
Universitätsbibliothek der Humboldt-Universität zu Berlin, Historische Sammlungen: 2942:tafe:'a':F8

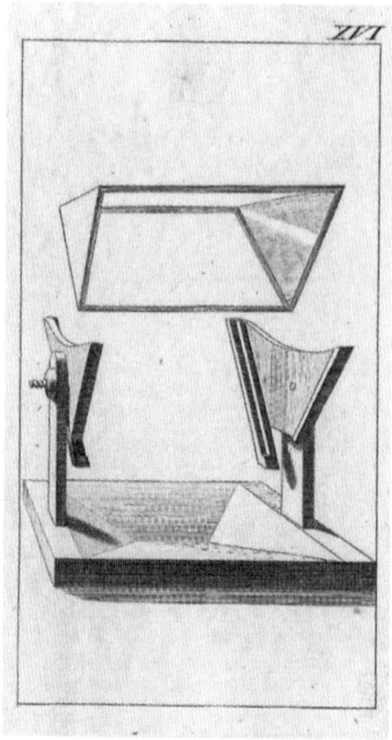

fig. 11

Goethe's water prism.
Plate XVI of Goethe's *Farbenlehre* shows the construction of a water prism. Goethe wanted to adjust the orientation of the prism such that rays of light could enter at an angle independent of the sun's position.
Universitätsbibliothek der Humboldt-Universität zu Berlin, Historische Sammlungen: 2942:tafe:'a':F8

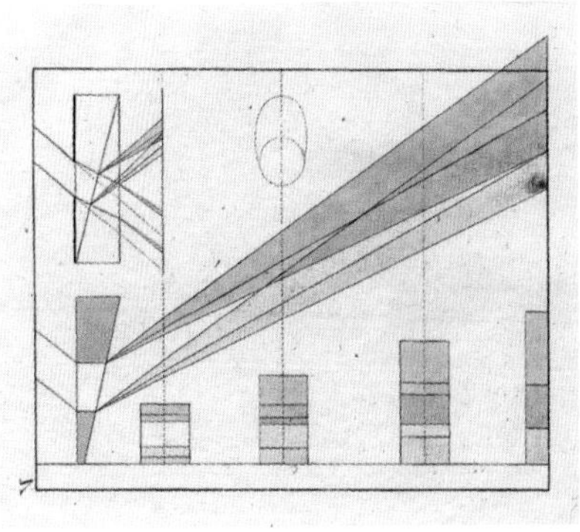

fig. 12

Newton's spectrum at various distances.
In Plate V of his *Farbenlehre*, Goethe shows how the spectral colours of sunlight change with distance. The green centre of Newton's spectrum only emerges at a distance of more than one metre.
Universitätsbibliothek der Humboldt-Universität zu Berlin, Historische Sammlungen: 2942:tafe:'a':F8, image rotated; the plate is available, for example, in Goethe 'Theory of Colors', plate VII before p. 207

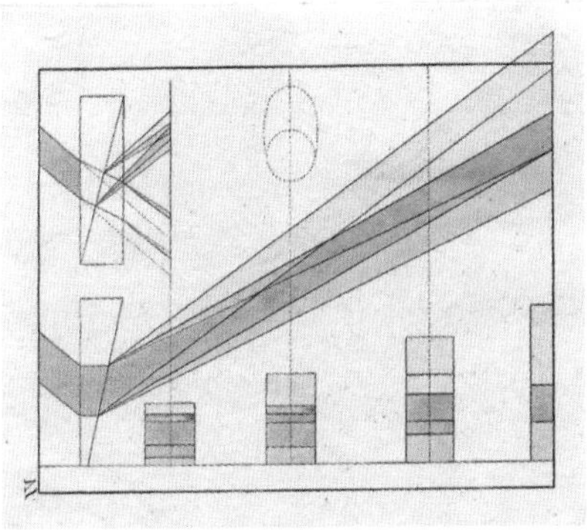

fig. 13

Goethe's spectrum at various distances.
In Plate VI of his *Farbenlehre*, Goethe shows how the spectral colours of darkness (that is, of a shadow) change with distance. This image is the polar opposite of the previous one.
Universitätsbibliothek der Humboldt-Universität zu Berlin, Historische Sammlungen: 2942:tafe:'a':F8, image rotated; the plate is available, for example, in Goethe 1988, plate VIII before p. 207

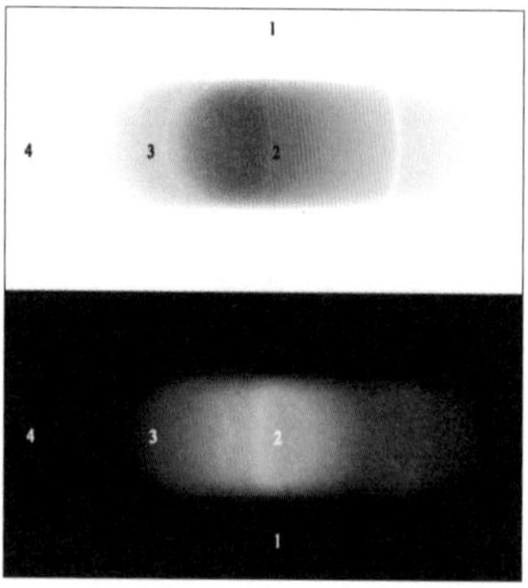

fig. 14

Polar inversion of infrared heat radiation

Top: When Matthias Rang and Johannes Grebe-Ellis repeated Herschel's experiment with modern means in Goethe's spectrum, they detected inverted relative temperatures. They began by measuring the temperature in the bright area above Goethe's spectrum (position 1). Moving the thermometer to the centre of Goethe's spectrum (position 2), they detected a decrease in temperature, which decreased further as they moved the thermometer into the turquoise area of the spectrum (position 3). Beyond that end of the spectrum (position 4), they found a temperature minimum; here we could speak of 'infraturquoise coldness radiation'.

Bottom: Herschel began by measuring the temperature in the dark area below Newton's spectrum (position 1). Moving the thermometer to the green centre of Newton's spectrum (position 2), he detected an increase in temperature, which increased further as he moved the thermometer into the red area of the spectrum (position 3). He found that the maximum temperature was beyond the red end of the spectrum (position 4), nowadays called infrared heat radiation.

Illustration by Olaf Müller; source: Müller 2017, p. 317, ill. 10

Similarly for the remaining experiments. Interestingly Newton's own theory predicts that all of his experiments can be inverted.[47] On the one hand this means that the inverted experiments cannot refute Newton's theory. On the other the overarching polarity of light and darkness in the realm of Newton's experiments spells bad news for his followers: Newton's theory is not the only theory that matches the data – and so his claim to have proven it experimentally is mistaken.[48] Any proof Newton could 'derive' from his experiments can be countered by means of inverted experiments with a structurally analogous counterproof of the theory that darkness, rather than light, is composed of colours of diverse refrangibility.[49] From this Goethe drew the philosophical conclusion that is still valid today: several distinct theories can be compatible with one and the same set of data; physics is less determinate than it appears.[50] Is the objectivity of physics perhaps in danger?[51]

Polarity beyond the visible parts of the spectra

I'll now turn to two further cases that demonstrate the success of a Goethean search for spectral polarity. One of these is from Goethe's time, the other from ours.[52]

Around 1800 William Herschel discovered infrared radiation beyond the red end of Newton's spectrum fig. 14 bottom but no radiation beyond the opposite end.[53] When Goethe's allies heard of this discovery, they sensed danger for his research programme.[54]

---

47 For proof see Müller 2015, pp. 209–16; an English sketch of the proof is offered in Müller 2016, Section 6.

48 Here is but one of Newton's statements in this regard: '*the Theory wich I propounded was evinced to me, not by inferring tis thus becouse not otherwise*, that is not by deducing it onely from a confutation of contrary suppositions, but *by deriving it from Experiments concluding positively & directly*' (Newton, letter to Oldenburg dated 6 July 1672 (see Turnbull 1959, p. 209); see also Newton 1984, pp. 86–7, Newton 1964, p. 5).

49 Goethe 1957b, p. 86; Goethe merely defended this theory for the sake of the argument (as a *reductio ad absurdum* of Newton's proofs). Joseph Reade, however, did champion the darkness theory (Reade 1814).

50 See the *locus classicus* (with deplorable lack of examples) in Quine 1975.

51 For details see Müller 2016, Sections 7 and 8.

52 For a more detailed account of both cases, see Müller 2018b, Section 4 and Müller 2018a, Section 3.

53 The *locus classicus* is Herschel 1800a and b.

54 Friedrich Schelling, letter to Goethe, dated 17 April 1801 (see Goethe 1947–2011: II.3, p. 135). For an English translation of this passage, see Müller 2018b, Section 4.

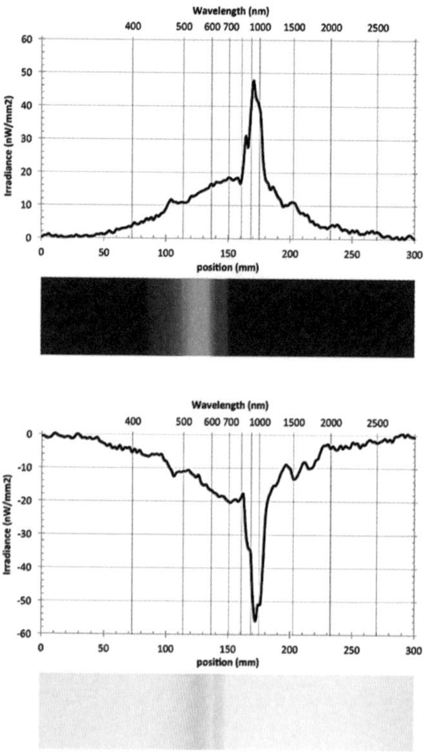

fig. 15

Experimental results from Newton's and in Goethe's spectrum.

The top graph shows the radiation detected in Newton's spectrum as a function of the position within the spectrum (given at the top in terms of wavelength). The polar results from Goethe's spectrum are shown in the bottom graph.

Image by Matthias Rang

How could Goethe's claim of spectral polarity be correct if the spectrum has an invisible extension at one end but not at the other? Can the spectral symmetry be salvaged in view of Herschel's results?

Such worries were soon assuaged. Johann Ritter, a talented young physicist, searched for effects observable beyond the other end of the spectrum. He was successful. On 22 February 1801 he discovered the effects of what is now known as ultraviolet light.[55] This discovery secured him a place in the annals of science. Ritter knew of the significance of his findings and how delighted Goethe would be on hearing about them. Instead of informing his colleagues in Jena, he packed his bags, headed straight for Weimar and met Goethe.[56] Goethe was captivated. After their meeting he composed a long letter to Ritter in which he suggested further experiments in line with his polar research programme.[57] Only recently have these experiments been carried out with results that fit Goethe's claims.[58] Parallel to Newton's spectrum, in Goethe's spectrum colour correlates with temperature – and changes of temperature continue beyond the visible part of the spectrum. Herschel measured a temperature maximum beyond the red end of Newton's spectrum (infrared heat radiation); a corresponding minimum has recently been measured beyond the turquoise end of Goethe's spectrum, as if there were infra-turquoise coldness radiation. fig. 14 top and 15

A multitude of colourful polarities

As I have outlined, Goethe pursued a polarity between light and darkness: exchanging these two poles in any of Newton's experiments leads to an inversion of the results, in terms of both colour and temperature. In the former case there is the opposition of colour and its complement, while in the latter there is the opposition of heat and coldness (as Kant had speculated).

In this final section I'll extend the concept of the polarity of light and darkness to chromatic colours. So far we have only

---

55 Ritter 1806. For a discussion in English, see Frercks et al. 2009.

56 For more details see Müller 2018b, Section 4 with references to the original literature.

57 Ritter published Goethe's letter shortly before his death (Goethe, letter to Ritter dated 7 March 1801 [see Ritter 1808, pp. 724–7]).

58 On this and the following, see Rang and Grebe-Ellis 2018.

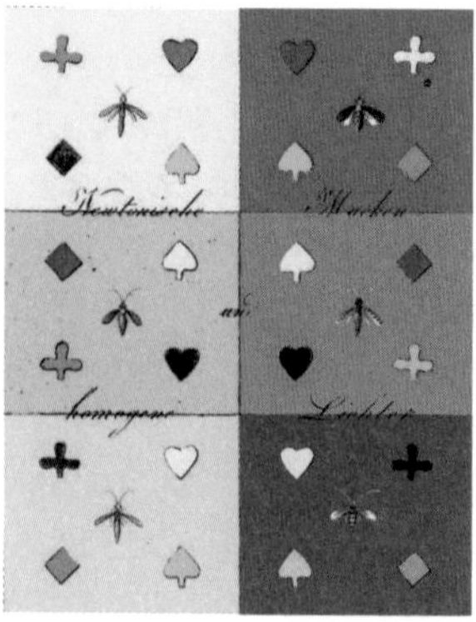

fig. 16

Goethe's prism template modernised.
When Newton peered through a prism at small black insects in monochromatic light, he noticed no changes in colour or shape (Newton, *'Opticks'*, p. 49 [Book I, Part I, Experiment 14]). Goethe mistakenly claimed that this experiment could be tested using plate XII of his *Farbenlehre*, where he presented pictures of insects on differently coloured backgrounds. Prismatic observations of these pictures obviously cannot reproduce Newton's results because the reflected light isn't monochromatic. Nonetheless the pictures are valuable as they can be used as templates for experiments in which coloured shapes are observed against a differently coloured background. Goethe can thus be seen as anticipating Nussbaumer's discovery of the disorderly spectra.
Illustration by Matthias Herder

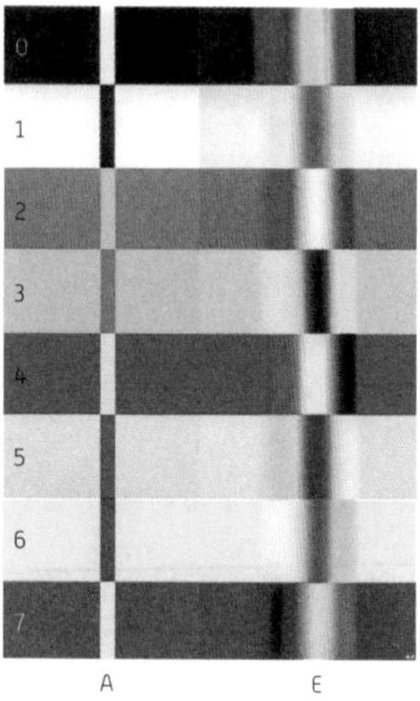

fig. 17

Photographs of the eight spectra.
The original contrast (left) seen through a water prism (right). All spectra are of the same size and differentiation.
Illustration by Ingo Nussbaumer

considered what happens if the achromatic complementary colours (that is, black and white) are decomposed with a prism; Newton's experiment featured a white ray of light in black surroundings fig. 12, while Goethe's inverted experiment involved a black shadow in white surroundings fig. 13. What happens if these experiments are conducted using chromatic complementary colours instead?

Goethe seems to have considered this question fig. 16, though he was unable to investigate it empirically for lack of suitable sources of coloured light.[59] Today these technological limitations have been overcome, and the matter has been taken up by painter and colour researcher Ingo Nussbaumer.[60] He investigated the following question: What happens if white light is replaced, for example, by yellow light and darkness by blue light (the complement of yellow)? Nussbaumer's experiments yield astonishing results. In every experiment new and different spectra emerge, but each of these spectra contains at least one of the two achromatic colours, white and black. A yellow ray of light against a blue background, for example, creates a spectrum of black, green, turquoise, white and magenta, and a complementary blue ray of light against a yellow background produces a spectrum of white, magenta, red, black and green:

Spectral results of a blue/yellow/blue contrast fig. 17, row no. 7	Spectral results of a yellow/blue/yellow contrast fig. 17, row no. 6
black	white
green	magenta
turquoise	red
white	black
magenta	green

The other pairs of complementary colours lead to four further spectra, which are similar to those we have just considered in terms of diversity, size and structure but again differ in colour:

59 Goethe 1957b, p. 98.

60 On these experiments, which are described here for the first time in English, see Nussbaumer 2008, pp. 200–6 et passim. I provide a brief overview of the matter in Müller 2008, Section V; for more details, see Müller 2013b and Müller 2015, §§III.5.11–III.5.16.

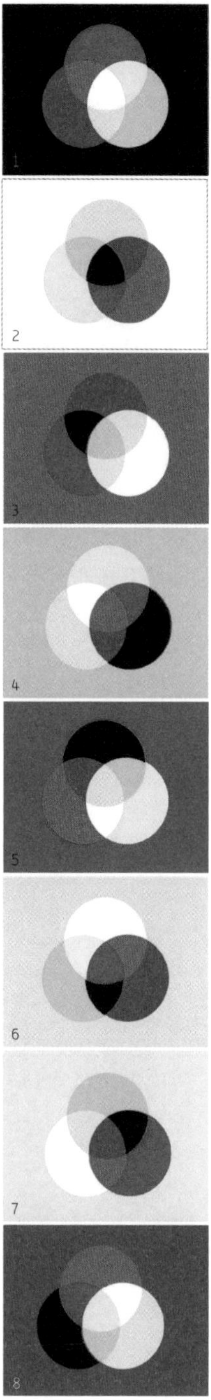

fig. 18

The eight colour-mixing diagrams.

Newton's additive rules of colour mixing show how the colours of his spectrum can be mixed to create white (in dark surroundings, image 1). In its inversion the colours of Goethe's spectrum are mixed to create black (in bright surroundings, fig. 18. 2). Colour mixing functions for the disorderly spectra as well (fig. 18.3–8)

Illustration by Ingo Nussbaumer

Spectral results of a magenta/green/magenta contrast fig. 17, row no. 2	Spectral results of a green/magenta/green contrast fig. 17, row no. 3
red	turquoise
yellow	blue
white	black
turquoise	red
blue	yellow

Spectral results of a red/turquoise/red contrast fig. 17, row no. 4	Spectral results of a turquoise/red/turquoise contrast fig. 17, row no. 5
magenta	green
white	black
yellow	blue
green	magenta
black	white

Nussbaumer calls these newly discovered spectra the 'disorderly' spectra, although they do exhibit a fascinating order fig. 18.

Outlook

To avoid a potential misunderstanding, none of the experiments I have presented refutes modern physics or Newtonian optics. The disorderly spectra of the previous section can be explained by optics and colorimetry. The decrease in temperature beyond the turquoise end of Goethe's spectrum follows from the law of conservation of energy.[61] Friends of science thus need not be concerned; there is no need to change physics.

Nonetheless the foregoing considerations should give us pause for thought. If Goethe's idea of spectral polarity can be extended this far, what would have happened if this thought had found more adherents and been systematically pursued during his lifetime? Would our physical theories look completely different? I don't know, but I find the question itself disconcerting enough.[62]

61 Rang and Grebe-Ellis 2018, Section 4.

62 I have defended an agnostic view on these counterfactuals in Müller 2016, pp. 342–3.

Bibliography

ADICKES, ERICH

Kant als Naturforscher: Band I (Vol. 1). Berlin: de Gruyter, 1924.

AEPIN, FRANZ ULRICH THEODOSIUS

Akademische Rede von der Aehnlichkeit der elektrischen und magnetischen Kraft. Leipzig: Gleditsch, 1760. (First appeared in German in 1759; the speech was given in Latin on 7 September 1757.)

BERGMAN, TORBERN

Physick beskrifning öfver jord-klotet, på cosmographiska sållskapets vágnar författad: Senare bandet (Vol. 1). Upsala: Edman, 1773. (First appeared in 1766.)

BERGMAN, TORBERN

Physick beskrifning öfver jord-klotet, på cosmographiska sållskapets vágnar författad: Senare bandet (Vol. 2). Upsala: Edman, 1774. (First appeared in 1766.)

BERGMAN, TORBERN

Physicalische Beschreibung der Erdkugel: Erster Band (Zwote vermehrte und verbesserte Auflage) (Vol. 1). Translated by Lampert Hinrich Röhl. Greifswald: Röse, 1780a. (First appeared in Swedish in 1766.)

BERGMAN, TORBERN

Physicalische Beschreibung der Erdkugel: Zweyter Band. (Zwote vermehrte und verbesserte Auflage) (Vol. 2). Translated by Lampert Hinrich Röhl. Greifswald: Röse, 1780b. (First appeared in Swedish in 1766.)

BJERKE, ANDRÉ

Neue Beiträge zu Goethes Farbenlehre: Erster Teil: Goethe contra Newton. Translated by Louise Funk. Stuttgart: Verlag Freies Geistesleben, 1963. (First appeared in Norwegian in 1961.)

BÖHLER, MICHAEL

'Scientific Writing between Tabloid Storytelling, Arcane Formulaic Hermetism, and Narrative Knowledge'. Journal for General Philosophy of Science 49, no. 4 (2018), pp. 551–67.

CHANG, HASOK

'Rumford and the Reflection of Radiant Cold: Historical Reflections and Metaphysical Reflexes'. Physics in Perspective 4, no. 2 (2002), pp. 127–69.

CHANG, HASOK

'Complementary Chemistry'. In Llored 2013, pp. 465–76.

DUCK, MICHAEL

'Introduction'. In Goethe 2016, pp. vii–xxviii.

ECKLE, JUTTA

'Olaf L. Müller: Mehr Licht: Goethe mit Newton im Streit um die Farben: Review'. Goethe-Jahrbuch 132 (2015), pp. 234–6.

FEEST, ULJANA, AND FRIEDRICH STEINLE (EDS)

Scientific Concepts and Investigative Practice. Studies in Knowledge Research series, vol. 3. Berlin: de Gruyter, 2012.

FRERCKS, JAN, HEIKO WEBER AND GERHARD WIESENFELDT

'Reception and Discovery: The Nature of Johann Wilhelm Ritter's Invisible Rays'. Studies in History and Philosophy of Science 40, no. 2 (2009), pp. 143–56.

GILBERT, WILLIAM

De magnete, magneticisque corporibus et de magno magnete tellure. London: Petrus Short, 1600.

GILBERT, WILLIAM

On the Loadstone and Magnetic Bodies, and on the Great Magnet the Earth. Translated by Fleury Mottelay. New York: Wiley, 1893. (First appeared in Latin in 1600.)

GOETHE, JOHANN WOLFGANG VON

'Leopoldina series'. Die Schriften zur Naturwissenschaft: Vollständige mit Erläuterungen versehene Ausgabe im Auftrage der Deutschen Akademie der Naturforscher Leopoldina. Edited by Jutta Eckle, Wolf von Engelhardt, Dorothea Kuhn, Rupprecht Matthaei, Irmgard Müller, Gisela Nickel, Thomas Nickol, Günther Schmid, Wilhelm Troll, Karl Lothar Wolf and Horst Zehe. Weimar: Böhlau, 1947–2011.

GOETHE, JOHANN WOLFGANG VON
Materialien zur Geschichte der Farbenlehre: Des zweiten Bandes erster, historischer Teil. Leopoldina series, I.6. Weimar: Böhlau, 1957a. (First appeared in 1810.)
GOETHE, JOHANN WOLFGANG VON
Erklärung der zu Goethes Farbenlehre gehörigen Tafeln. Leopoldina series, I.7, pp. 41–114. Weimar: Böhlau, 1957b. (First appeared in 1810.)
GOETHE, JOHANN WOLFGANG VON
'Theory of Colors: Didactic Section'. In Goethe, Scientific Studies. Translated and edited by Douglas Miller. New York: Suhrkamp, 1988, pp. 157–298. (First appeared in German in 1808.)
GOETHE, JOHANN WOLFGANG VON
Exposure of Newton's Theory: A Polemic on Newton's Theory of Light and Colour. Translated by Michael Duck and Michael Petry. London: Imperial College Press, 2016. (First appeared in German in 1810.)
HENLEY, ERNEST M., AND ALEJANDRO GARCÍA
Subatomic Physics. New Jersey: World Scientific, 2007. (First appeared in 1976.)
HERSCHEL, WILLIAM
'Experiments on the Solar, and on the Terrestrial Rays that Occasion Heat; with a Comparative View of the Laws to which Light and Heat, or Rather the Rays which Occasion them, are Subject, in order to Determine whether they are the Same, or Different. Part I'. Philosophical Transactions 90, no. 2 (1800a), pp. 293–326.
HERSCHEL, WILLIAM
'Experiments on the Solar, and on the Terrestrial Rays that Occasion Heat; with a Comparative View of the Laws to which Light and Heat, or Rather the Rays which Occasion them, are Subject, in order to Determine whether they are the Same, or Different. Part II'. Philosophical Transactions 90, no. 3 (1800b), pp. 437–538.
HOLTSMARK, TORGER
'Newton's experimentum crucis Reconsidered'. American Journal of Physics 38, no. 10 (1970), pp. 1229–35.
KANT, IMMANUEL
'Versuch den Begriff der negativen Größen in die Weltweisheit einzuführen'. In Kant's gesammelte Schriften. Band II. Erste Abtheilung: Werke. Zweiter Band: Vorkritische Schriften II. 1757–1777. Akademieausgabe, Berlin: Reimer, 1912, pp. 165–204. (First appeared in 1763.)
KANT, IMMANUEL
Kritik der reinen Vernunft. Edited by Raymund Schmidt. Hamburg: Meiner, 1976. (First appeared in 1781 ('A') and in 1787 ('B'); references according to the margin numbers, which point to the A or B edition.)
KANT, IMMANUEL
'Attempt to Introduce the Concept of Negative Magnitudes into Philosophy (1763)'. In Kant, Theoretical Philosophy, 1755–1770. Translated and edited by David Walford. Cambridge: Cambridge University Press, 2002, pp. 203–41. (First appeared in German in 1763.)
KLEINKNECHT, KONRAD (ED.)
Quanten. Schriftenreihe der Heisenberg-Gesellschaft series, vol. 1. Stuttgart: Hirzel, 2013.
KLINGER, KERRIN, AND MATTHIAS MÜLLER
'Goethe und die Camera obscura'. Goethe-Jahrbuch 125 (2008), pp. 219–38.
KÖTTER, RUDOLF
'Müller, Olaf L.: Mehr Licht: Goethe mit Newton im Streit um die Farben: Review'. Journal for General Philosophy of Science 48, no. 1 (2017), pp. 155–60.
LICHTENBERG, GEORG CHRISTOPH
Über eine neue Methode, die Natur und die Bewegung der elektrischen Materie zu erforschen. ['Lichtenbergsche Figuren']. Edited by Herbert Pupke and translated by Ludwig Christian Lichtenberg and Friedrich Kries. Leipzig: Akademische Verlagsgesellschaft, 1956.
LICHTENBERG, GEORG CHRISTOPH
'Zweite Abhandlung über eine neue Methode, die Natur und die Bewegung der elektrischen Materie zu erforschen. Eingereicht am 19. Dezember 1778'. In Lichtenberg 1956, pp. 31–45. (First appeared in Latin in 1779; first appeared in German in 1806.)

LLORED, JEAN-PIERRE (ED.)
The Philosophy of Chemistry: Practices, Methodologies, and Concepts. Newcastle upon Tyne: Cambridge Scholars Publishing, 2013.
MÜLLER, OLAF
'Die Neuvermessung der Farbenwelt durch Ingo Nussbaumer: Eine kleine Sensation'. In Nussbaumer 2008, pp. 11–20. (Available at: http://nbn-resolving.de/urn:nbn:de:kobv:11-10090241.)
MÜLLER, OLAF
'Colour Spectral Counterpoints: Case Study on Aesthetic Judgement in the Experimental Sciences'. In Nussbaumer 2010, pp. 150–69. (Available at http://nbn-resolving.de/urn:nbn:de:kobv:11-100180762.)
MÜLLER, OLAF
'Goethes Pech mit Schelling: Optimistische Blicke auf ein ideengeschichtliches Fiasko'. In Corriero and Dezi (eds), Nature and Realism in Schelling's Philosophy. Turin: Accademia University Press, 2013a, pp. 131–85. (Available at: http://nbn-resolving.de/urn:nbn:de:kobv:11-100228398.)
MÜLLER, OLAF
'Newton, Goethe und die Entdeckung neuer Farbspektren am Ende des Zwanzigsten Jahrhunderts'. In Vogt and Karliczek (eds), Erkenntniswert Farbe. Jena: Ernst-Haeckel-Haus, 2013b, pp. 45–82.
MÜLLER, OLAF
Mehr Licht: Goethe mit Newton im Streit um die Farben. Frankfurt am Main: Fischer, 2015.
MÜLLER, OLAF
'Prismatic Equivalence: A New Case of Underdetermination. Goethe vs. Newton on the Prism Experiments'. British Journal for the History of Philosophy 24, no. 2 (2016), pp. 323–47.
MÜLLER, OLAF
'Goethes größte wissenschaftliche Entdeckung: Über eine verblüffende Symmetrie bei den Spektralfarben'. In Schlette et al. 2017, pp. 269–317.
MÜLLER, OLAF
'Goethe's Polarity of Light and Darkness'. Journal for General Philosophy of Science 49, no. 4 (2018a), pp. 581–98.
MÜLLER, OLAF
'Goethe and Ritter'. In Vine (ed.), Experience Colour: An Exhibition by Nora Löbe and Matthias Rang. Stourbridge: Ruskin Mill Land Trust, 2018b, pp. 150–9.
NAKAJIMA, HIDETO
'Two Kinds of Modification Theory of Light: Some New Observations on the Newton-Hooke Controversy of 1672 concerning the Nature of Light'. Annals of Science 41, no. 3 (1984), pp. 261–78.
NEWTON, ISAAC
'A letter of Mr. Isaac Newton, Professor of the Mathematicks in the University of Cambridge; containing his New Theory about Light and Colors'. Philosophical Transactions 6, no. 80 (1671/2), pp. 3075–87.
NEWTON, ISAAC
'Optics: or, a Treatise of the Reflections, Refractions, Inflections and Colours of Light'. In Newton, Opera quae exstant omnia: Band 4 (Vol. 4). Stuttgart: Frommann, 1964, pp. 1–264. (First appeared in 1704.)
NEWTON, ISAAC
The Unpublished First Version of Isaac Newton's Cambridge Lectures on Optics, 1670–1672. Edited by Derek Thomas Whiteside. Cambridge: Cambridge University Library, 1973.
NEWTON, ISAAC
'Lectiones opticae – Optical Lectures'. In Shapiro 1984, pp. 45–279.
NUSSBAUMER, INGO
Zur Farbenlehre: Entdeckung der unordentlichen Spektren. Vienna: Edition Splitter, 2008.
NUSSBAUMER, INGO
Restraint versus Intervention: Painting as Alignment. Nuremberg: Verlag für moderne Kunst, 2010.

QUINE, WILLARD VAN ORMAN
'On Empirically Equivalent Systems of the World'. Erkenntnis 9, no. 3 (1975), pp. 313–28.
RANG, MATTHIAS
Phänomenologie komplementärer Spektren. Phänomenologie in den Naturwissenschaften series, vol. 9. Berlin: Logos, 2015.
RANG, MATTHIAS, AND JOHANNES GREBE-ELLIS
'Power Area Density in Inverse Spectra'. Journal for General Philosophy of Science 49, no. 4 (2018), pp. 515–23.
RANG, MATTHIAS, AND OLAF MÜLLER
'Newton in Grönland: Das umgestülpte experimentum crucis in der Streulichtkammer'. philosophia naturalis 46, no. 1 (2009), pp. 61–114. (Available at http://nbn-resolving.de/urn:nbn:de:kobv:11-100187051.)
READE, JOSEPH
'Dr. Reade's New Experiments on Light'. The Monthly Magazine 252, vol. 37, no. 2 (1.3.1814), pp. 105–7.
RITTER, JOHANN WILHELM
'Bemerkungen zu Herschel's neueren Untersuchungen über das Licht'. In Ritter, Physisch-Chemische Abhandlungen in chronologischer Folge: Zweyter Band (Vol. 2). Leipzig: Reclam, 1806, pp. 81–107. (Lecture at 'Naturforschende Gesellschaft zu Jena', spring 1801.)
RITTER, JOHANN WILHELM (ED.)
'Schreiben des Geh. Rath von Goethe an J. W. Ritter'. Journal für die Chemie, Physik und Mineralogie 6, no. 4 (1808), pp. 719–29, 759.
SÄLLSTRÖM, PEHR
Monochromatic Shadow Rays: A Film about Experiments on the Rehabilitation of Darkness. Stuttgart: Edition Waldorf, 2010. (DVD.)
SCHELLING, FRIEDRICH WILHELM JOSEPH VON
'Von der Weltseele, eine Hypothese der höheren Physik zur Erklärung des allgemeinen Organismus'. In Schelling, Sämmtliche Werke: Erste Abtheilung, zweiter Band, 1797, 1798 (Vol. 2). Stuttgart: Cotta, 1857, pp. 345–583. (First appeared 1798.)
SCHLETTE, MAGNUS, THOMAS FUCHS AND ANNA MARIA KIRCHNER (EDS)
Anthropologie der Wahrnehmung. Heidelberg: Winter, 2017.
SHAPIRO, ALAN E. (ED.)
The Optical Papers of Isaac Newton, Volume I: The Optical Lectures, 1670–1672. Cambridge: Cambridge University Press, 1984.
SHAPIRO, ALAN E.
'The Gradual Acceptance of Newton's Theory of Light and Color, 1672–1727'. Perspectives on Science 4, no. 1 (1996), pp. 59–140.
STEINLE, FRIEDRICH
'Goals and Fates of Concepts: The Case of Magnetic Poles'. In Feest and Steinle 2012, pp. 105–25.
STEINLE, FRIEDRICH
'Wie Begriffe entstehen: Der Fall der Elektrodynamik'. In Kleinknecht 2013, pp. 45–96.
TURNBULL, HERBERT WESTREN (ED.)
The Correspondence of Isaac Newton. Volume I: 1661–1675. Cambridge: Cambridge University Press, 1959.
WIESENFELDT, GERHARD, AND OLAF BREIDBACH
'"Könnte nicht also auch die Erdkugel ein großer Turmalin sein?" Ein Kristall, Lichtenberg und die Polaritätsdiskussion vor 1800'. Sudhoffs Archiv 96, no. 1 (2012), pp. 95–109.
ZEMPLÉN, GÁBOR
An Eye for Optical Theory? Newton's Rejection of the Modificationist Tradition and Goethe's Modificationist Critique of Newton. Dissertation at the Department of Philosophy and History of Science, University of Technology and Economics, Budapest, 2001.

Wilhelm Lindemann

Gemstones – The Crystalline
From Natural Sciences Paradigm to Art Symbol

Introduction

Gemstones are cultural phenomena. The term itself indicates human involvement, namely dealing with stones that man qualifies as 'precious'. The German term *edel* denotes the social status of nobility, implies an ethical meaning and only points in the tertiary definition towards an economic value. Gemology, in this respect, as a partial discipline of mineralogy because of its very narrow focus, can barely enlighten the sophisticated interaction with this millennial natural object whose conspicuousness ascribes symbolic meaning. What today is connoted as symbolic content in the term 'gemstone' is, even viewed subjectively, cultivated through dynamic long-term cultural practice. Today's value standards only reflect the rationality of the market and are anything but objective. Since gemstones do not have a practical value, their value depends upon and presupposes the historically accumulated symbolic content. In the following I will attempt to, from my perspective, follow the primary continuities in the development of the symbolic content of gemstones. This will transpire in two primary aspects: on the one hand the cultural practice, on the other that of natural science. Here we will only scrutinise the Mediterranean-European cultural area spanning from Antiquity to the nineteenth century. The target area in my reflection is, in particular, the crystal within its evolving conflict between industrial prototype and art symbol.[1]

1 The term *crystalline* as an art symbol was coined by Regine Prange. See Regine Prange, *Das Kristalline als Kunstsymbol: Bruno Taut und Paul Klee*, Hildesheim, Zurich and New York, 1991.

The crystal is presented and interpreted, within the framework of the ThinkingJewellery Symposium,[2] from two significant perspectives – as a material and as an art object. We have to keep in mind, however, that, contrary to present-day glamorised mythos, it was viewed and used in alternative contexts throughout its history. In historical books about rocks, for example, gemstones were depicted as special cases of minerals, to which especially ores and coloured earths and so forth belonged and to which a considerable economic benefit is attributed. This deserves special mention because crystals, like salt, have been commodities since the Late Stone Age.[3] Even the cultural sciences, which have documented the history of the crystal as an artefact since Antiquity, did not have an entirely unclouded view. Several facts support this:

- The term 'precious stone' did not take on more reliable, systematic contours until the seventeenth century. Gemology, to which the power of definition is attributed today, is a child of the turn of the nineteenth century.
- Also for historical epochs, the crystal is primarily assigned a decorative function in the sense of a modern understanding of ornamentation – although decorating oneself as an act of profane embellishment is itself a child of the Modern Era.
- The 'gemstone' is accredited ex post with material characteristics of Antiquity, such as 'sparkle', which objectively the gemstone could only rarely display since the necessary techniques required to produce the effect were not yet available.
- The valuation system formed by today's culture with value standards shaped by the capitalist exchange of goods is transferred to historical epochs and cultures which cultivated and maintain not only other standards of valuation but also other practices.

The individual aspects simultaneously represent diverging societal interests that portray the respective points of view of the societal protagonists. Moreover these viewpoints can rarely be clearly distinguished from one another. They penetrate each other – but sometimes economic, sometimes technical-scientific, sometimes aesthetic positions are at the forefront.

---

2 Parts of this text were presented as a lecture at the ThinkingJewellery XI symposium.

3 In the early modern history of crystallography – for example, in the case of Robert Boyle – salting was of great importance.

In order to clarify the term, it should first be said that minerals and crystals are regarded as natural objects, whereas precious stones are regarded as minerals, cultural objects and artefacts processed in some way by humans. The latter are listed historically (also in the present day) in inventories of gemology and trade, among other things, with the attribute 'noble'.[4] In international language usage it is succinctly assessed as 'precious', valuable or expensive. Also the art of stone cutting – if the crystal is used as a material of mimetic illustration – should be considered separately as part of sculpture:[5] It has been part of art since the Renaissance. Forms of the stone cut such as ancient magical objects of little craftsmanship, or heraldic and authenticating stones are included in this. In this context it is initially unimportant whether an object is classified as an art object.

Gemstones to the end of the Middle Age

At the outset of Greek-Roman antiquity

In Greek-Roman natural sciences literature, gemstones rarely receive special classification and are grouped instead in the mineral realm. In most cases Theophrast (ca. 371–ca. 287 BC) is considered the author of gemology.[6] In his book *Peri Lithion* (About Stones),

---

4 The German term *edel* (precious) becomes historically and sociologically concrete and confers an initially kingly qualification: nobility. In religious-ritual or ceremonial practice, the term was transferred to the stone itself – where so-called contact relics were used in Christian rituals, during which the person touching the holy stone becomes holy. This also happened among the gentry. This denotation has no bearing upon the physical characteristics of the material, such as size, colour, transparency etc., or how the stone is worked.

5 Giorgio Vasari postulates in *Proemio di tutta l'opera* [Foreword to the Entire Works] in 1568 (reissue: Giorgio Vasari, *Kunstgeschichte und Kunsttheorie*, Berlin, 2004, p. 29) that '*almighty God made man, and this was the first sculpture. It is said that the sculpture is comprised of many related arts and gathers many such others within itself, such as painters, flat relief artists, the working of clay, wax, stucco, wood, ivory, the casting of metal, all types of carving or engraving, the deep and relief cutting of gemstones and metals and many other techniques that surpass painting in both quantity and expertise.*'

6 The book, written in Greek, with the introduction and commentary translated into English, published by Ohio State University, Columbus, OH, 1956, is available on the homepage of the jewellery company Farlang (www.farlang.com/books/theophrastus-on-stones-translation-into-english). The book is not a 'gemstone book' but rather deals with stone as a material. However, the translation and commentary clearly mirror today's perspective on gemstones. Theophrast, a student and successor of Aristotle's at the Peripatetic Academy, discusses the subject well under his customary theoretical standard; his apparent position at the outset is Aristotelian physics.

the Aristotelian student only briefly discusses the origin of minerals and describes them as a mixture of the elements water and earth in particular that converge under certain processes (confluence, filtering). Since the element earth, like all elements according to Aristotelian opinion, usually appears as a compound in nature, coloured materials such as metals are inevitably involved in the colouring of stones. The coincidence of the antagonistic qualities attributed to the elements (warmth, cold, drought, moisture)[7] causes, according to Aristotelian belief, chemical reactions leading to the creation of new substances.[8] Even if such processes are not dealt with concretely by Theophrast, the author lets it show in some places that there is already an astonishing practical knowledge of metallurgy during this epoch. Theophrast mentions finds of natural chrysocolla, which was already used for soldering in ancient times.[9]

Gemstone finds are, in the literature of Antiquity, generally mentioned in connection with the mining industry's acquisition of ores (iron, copper, gold, silver) or with the extraction of minerals used for the production of paint or medication. Through the Middle Ages, at least in Europe, there were presumably no systematic attempts at gemstone mining. No form of specific prospection is mentioned either. In the Alpine region prospection seems to have developed in the fifteenth century in connection with the Venetian glass industry and the gemstone cutting that flourished in the northern Italian city states.[10]

---

7 Corresponding properties of the four elements:

	dry	*moist*
warm	fire	air
cold	earth	water

8 A short but competent introduction into Aristotelian chemistry by Gernot Böhme, *Alternativen der Wissenschaft*, Frankfurt/Main, 1980, pp. 101–20.

9 See Harald Othmar Lenz, *Gemeinnützige Naturgeschichte*, vol. 5, Gotha, 1835, p. 21, note 71: 'Chrysocolla means gold solder – Theophrast apparently understands malachite at this point, which finds itself dusty. Our gold workers solder the gold with an alloy of gold, silver and copper; in any case so do the ancients, at least there is no trace of them using other materials. Now that malachite melted with coal easily gives a very pure copper, it was quite natural to use it to obtain the pure copper needed for gold soldering.'

10 See Rudolf Werner Soukup, *Chemie in Österreich: Von den Anfängen bis zum Ende des 18. Jahrhunderts*, Vienna, Cologne and Weimar, 2007, pp. 80–1. The author dates the earliest known 'prospecting book' of 1470; the first mention of emerald mining in the Alps appears in 1669.

Aside from several texts[11] on natural philosophy by Aristotle, it is Plato's *Timaios* that for the most part defines the natural-philosophical concept of the four-element theory. Hundreds of gemstone books had been written prior to Albertus Magnus's *De Mineralibus* around AD 1250; however, since a theoretically substantiated examination of minerals did not exist, the origin of crystals remained mostly vague and speculative. Pliny (Caius Plinius Secundus) discusses the compression of *'liquid substances under the Earth through heat'*[12] and refers to the genesis of the quartz rock crystal: *'An opposite cause produces rock-crystal; for it is hardened by intense cold. At any rate, this mineral is found only where the winter snows freeze solid and it is undoutbtedly a kind of ice, which ist the reason fo the Greek term* krystallos.'[13]

It is Albertus Magnus who takes up the Aristotelian thread again in his depiction of its genesis, when he says that through extraordinary cold at great heights, the crystalline substance coagulates through the removal of moisture in extreme dryness and solar radiation, whereby the transparency of water and air is preserved as the essential quality in the crystal.[14] Albertus Magnus adopts not only the natural philosophical tradition but also the Arabian authors of the Middle Ages such as Avicenna. Including the alchemical sources, he critically discusses them on the back of his own observation and reflection of nature with the intention of a new scientific justification.

The mineralogical knowledge of Antiquity appears initially – at least if you trace the written records – to be rather limited. However, the subtle knowledge of metallurgy, and the production of alloys, colouring techniques or the production of glass that Theophrast, among others, already possessed, points rather to our hitherto little researched terrain. That this is the case may have a number of reasons:

- It deals with manual workmanship practices obtained through empirical knowledge that was not at all or just marginally

---

11 See *Physik* and especially *Vom Werden und Vergehen, Über den Himmel und Meteorologie*.

12 C. Plinius Secundus, *Naturalis Historiae Liber XXXVII*, 23 in Pliny the Elder, Natural History - a Selection, London 1991.

13 Ibid.

14 Albertus Magnus, *De Mineralibus,* Tractate II, Chap. II. Especially worth reading is book I of Albertus Magnus, *Book of Minerals*, transl. Dorothy Wyckoff, Oxford, 1967.

conceived by the academic scientific establishment and writings of Antiquity.[15]

- The knowledge was displaced through cultural or political processes or ideologically driven restrictions.
- Existing sources are, even in the present, scientifically researched to a limited extent only.

This topic cannot be gone into in any greater depth as it would go beyond the scope of this article. This notwithstanding, a few comments can be made. On the one hand there are indications that the lithotherapy by means of mineral medication used by Dioscorides, for example, was replaced in Late Antiquity by magical healing practices with precious stones.[16] On the other hand a meta study submitted by Carmélia Opsomer, in which she examined 28,000 publicised pharmaceutical prescriptions dating from the first to the tenth centuries AD, emphatically proves the high level of empirically based knowledge of medicines, but also the fact that gemstones or minerals play virtually no role in pharmacy.[17] This supports the view that in lithotherapy 'gemstones' are almost always used as magic objects and at best cause the placebo

---

15 This relative disregard of manual craftsmanship knowledge in Antiquity continues in the Middle Ages, manifesting as a dissociation of knowledge systems into *artes liberales* within the newly founded universities and in the dissemination of verbal knowledge within the craft guilds. It wasn't until the end of the eighteenth century of the Modern Era that natural sciences became established in universities. Up until then natural sciences research took place, with few exceptions, through private funding within the courts of the high nobility or within the institutions supported by the high nobility or the Church. In comparison see Fritz Krafft, 'Die Schwere der Luft in der Diskussion des 17. Jahrhunderts: Otto von Guericke', in Wim Klever (ed.), *Die Schwere der Luft in der Diskussion des 17. Jahrhunderts* (vol. 29 of Wolfenbuetteler Arbeiten zur Barockforschung), Wiesbaden, 1997, pp. 135–9.

16 According to Rainer A. Müller, *Edelsteinmedizin im Mittelalter: Die Entwicklung der spätantiken und mittelalterlichen Lithotherapie unter besonderer Berücksichtigung des Konrad von Megenberg*, Munich, 1984, pp. 4ff. The author critically argues with the Christian tradition of lithotherapy and evaluates the state of Arabian medicine as more positive. '*Its unrestricted merit was, moreover, that it attempted to eliminate the magical-irrational elements of lithotherapy and gave preference to the administration of minerals in powders and salves. These advances towards empiricism and rationality ebbed again and had nothing to do with currents within Arabic medicine but with the influence of Christianity, which, under the cover of mysticism, allowed for a resurgence of pagan-occult practices and repressed medicine to its former, ancient level.*' Ibid., p. 9.

17 Carmélia Opsomer, *Index de la pharmacopée du Ier au Xe siècle*, 2 vols., Hildesheim, 1989.

effect. Moreover the Hellenistic academies in Alexandria and Athens between AD 290 and 529 (the closure of the Athenian academy was carried out by Justinian) were massively suppressed through political measures which, from the reign of Constantine I on, were connected with the elevation of Christianity to a state religion. The scholars were expelled to Syria and then to the Islamic domain. In the centuries thereafter the legacy of Greek-Roman Antiquity fertilised the sciences of the Muslim Orient. It was not until the eleventh/twelfth century that the works of Plato and Aristotle, in addition to oriental knowledge, primarily from Arabian sources, were translated into Latin. This is especially true for mathematics, astronomy, medicine and chemistry. The emergence of 'alchemy'[18] is placed within this Alexandrian Epoch of the Middle Ages and the Renaissance. There is much to suggest that part of the empirical knowledge was handed down in proto-industrial and craft practices as well as in alchemistic practice, but especially in the Renaissance it was also infiltrated by esoteric views. Berthelot's[19] commendable research brought some of these to the surface in the late nineteenth century, although the author has only come close to re-evaluating the material in the sense of early chemical knowledge. Also later scientific work qualifies the ancient practice of dyeing gemstones as forgery in the sense of a criminal act, although at that time there was no market at all for such a crime.[20] An understanding of authenticity or originality of any kind had not yet been developed.

Concerning the symbolic meaning of gemstones to the end of the Middle Ages

The symbolic significance of gemstones in modern times also has a millennium of prehistory in which the modern gemstone symbol –

---

18 Concerning the etymology of the term, see Franz Strunz, *Beiträge und Skizzen zur Geschichte der Naturwissenschaften*, Hamburg and Leipzig, 1909, p. 3. Strunz connects the term 'alchemy' from the Arabian prefixes *al* and *chemeía* to the old name from Egypt *chemi*. 'This linguistic deduction gains in status as, especially for the Egyptians, chemical practice was gaining in popularity among cults and religious adoration; in other words it was a 'holy art', *a hagia technê*.'

19 See especially M. Berthelot, *Collection des anciens alchimistes grecs*, 3 vols., Paris, 1888, reprint: Osnabrück, 1967; and idem, *Die Chemie im Altertum und im Mittelalter*, foreword and commentary by Franz Strunz, Vienna, 1909, reprint: Hildesheim, 2003. Also Strunz 1909 (note 18), and Franz Strunz, *Albertus Magnus*, Vienna and Leipzig, 1926.

20 According to Dieter Helm, *Farben und Färben von Edelsteinen in der Antike*, dissertation, Frankfurt/Main, 1978.

prenatally, so to speak – was pre-formed. In this longest stage of gemstone culture, there is a diverse practice of using gemstones. However, as the ancient world proves with its highly flourishing written scientific culture, it is by no means possible to speak of a scientific 'gemology'. Until the end of the Middle Ages, there were hundreds of gemstone books in which the magical healing effects of the stones were primarily discussed. These were usually constructed according to the encyclopaedic models of Pliny Secundus or Isidore of Seville and list a variety of provenances and their composition according to different stones. However, they were mostly based on information from the originals and rarely on the expertise of the authors. Since there was no scientific basis yet, there can be no classification of stones or a well-founded systematics, so that the nomenclature is also extremely unreliable.

Gemstones usually do not play a special role in natural philosophy. The more elaborate authors of Antiquity and the Middle Ages dealt with them alongside metals, mineral colours and other materials rather implicitly on the basis of the theory of elements. The first scientific attempt at a systematic classification into Aristotelian physics was reserved for Albertus Magnus in the thirteenth century. Such scientific experiments remained the exception until well into modern times.

In the 'latency phase' of the modern gemstone symbol, there are different practices in dealing with minerals. Thus they have magical, religious-cultic, authenticating and political functions, or serve as luxury items.

In the magical or documentary context, the artful design has no meaning. In the religious or cultic field as well as with political representative objects, on the other hand, there is an extraordinary skill in gemstone carving. They do not have a decorative function in the modern sense of decoration, as their profane use is frowned upon, if not forbidden. The sequence of the list of practices is random, the individual aspects even relatively blurred, since they interpenetrate each other and usually appear cumulatively. Especially since the Middle Ages, there has been an increasing convergence of the interpretational systems. This process begins in the Mediterranean-European cultural circle with the rise of Christianity to state religion in the fourth century AD. This leads for a whole millennium to the unification of political and ecclesiastical power on the basis of Christian doctrine. The ancient natural philosophical tradition is nearly entirely suppressed as pagan.

The supremacy of biblical cosmology as a God-given creationistic history is settled. The Book of Nature is the Bible – even if in the High Middle Ages it encountered Arabic and, through this, also ancient knowledge.

The Constantinian epoch brought a ban on the 'magic gems', which had previously been popular in the Mediterranean region. Constantine's successors introduced imperial rights of reservation for the wearing of precious stones.

Due to their effectiveness to the present day, the five practices mentioned above will be expanded.

Gemstones as magical objects: Magical practices are not only found in archaic cults. This includes all practices associated with the assumption that a magical object has a hoped-for effect. Stones have magic power as talismans or amulets. The antique 'magic gems' were first disseminated in Egypt and above all in the eastern Mediterranean area. From there they spread throughout the entire Roman Empire. They were used, for example, in medicine and worn as love or defence charms. Later they gained considerable prestige in medieval gemstone medicine and modern esotericism, but also as a gift in today's usual form of a love charm, in which love or gratitude is expected in return.

Because of the exceptional dispersal and diverse possibilities in their application, the well-researched magical gems[21] that stem from Ptolemaic Egypt deserve a closer look. Simone Michel points out the good state of knowledge of the magical practices in Alexandria, Egypt:

'Numerous ancient texts give guidance on the time and method of making and wearing amulets, whose effectiveness is mostly based on the synthesis of a certain material, image and magic formula [logos] as well as a complicated consecration process [practice].'[22]

Michel's research of 2,600 magical gems shows that the variety of the stones – even if they are almost exclusively lithic – is of secondary significance:

'Generally the individual colours received a higher valuation than the material itself, indicating that the "effectiveness" of the amulet is more dependent upon the interplay of colours,

21 In comparison see especially Simone Michel, *Die magischen Gemmen: Zu Bildern und Zauberformeln auf geschnittenen Steinen der Antike und Neuzeit*, Berlin, 2004.

22 Ibid., pp. 3–4.

appearance and inscription than on the bond to the variety of stone.'[23] Of particular importance is the dedication of the gem by the pictorial motif, which mostly symbolises a deity and which assigns it to the sphere of the holy, as well as by an inscription with a magical meaning. Of extraordinary importance is the magical charge, which Michel proved by means of magical papyri and ritual consecration acts performed by 'knowledgeable' magicians, giving the gem the desired effect.

'The symbolic usage of objects is subject to an elaborated code. The relationship between the significant and the signified is never entirely random. However, there is an exception, namely sacral objects. They share the characteristic arbitrariness through verbal signs. Any material object can generally be seen as, and experienced as, being representational of the holy. Its primary intended use does not limit its usage as a carrier of sacral meaning; this also applies to the previously named and arbitrarily selected example. From stones spread throughout the entire world as cult objects, through the act of transformation, and common food products like bread and wine in the Catholic Mass, to the embodiment of the body and blood of Jesus Christ, the double-bladed axe was considered an attribute of the godly not only by the Cretans but by other populaces of Antiquity too; even airplanes were, within the framework of the Melanesian cargo culture, venerated as the magical vehicles of arisen ancestors.'[24]

Even though the magic gems are rooted spiritually in the world of the regeneration belief in transmigration and rebirth, which is at home in the ancient Egyptian tradition but also in Christian Gnosis, they are rarely found as burial objects. As protective spells, love charms or medicines, they are personal objects of daily use for the living. Equipped with a communicative function, however, they on no account serve as decorative jewellery objects.

---

23 Ibid., p. 225; according to Michel's determination, most of these gems have a representative reference to a particular God, who in turn is represented with a certain colour. 'The preferred use of lapis lazuli for Aphrodite Anadyomene explains itself out of her function as moon goddess as well as her equal status with Isis and Hathor; blue was the colour of the moon, associated with moisture and water; Hathor was considered the "mistress of the blue stones". The stone lapis lazuli and the colour blue emphasised the Egyptian heritage of a god, thus it is used for Serapis; he is motivic and historically equivalent to Zeus (Jupiter), who is bound to the milky-white Chalcedon' (ibid., pp. 225–6).

24 The ethnologist Karl-Heinz Kohl in his historical cross-cultural research (Karl-Heinz Kohl, *Die Macht der Dinge: Geschichte und Theorie sakraler Objekte*, Munich, 2003, p. 157).

'The execution of paintings and engravings that are evaluated as artistically unpretentious is also an often-cited indication of the minimal material value of the amulet and the users' low position in society. Generally there was little or no artistic requirement, since these objects were not worn openly as jewellery but hidden, secret and close to the body, in order to achieve the maximum effect, upon which the artistic aspect had no bearing. Creativity was also not in demand when designing the motifs due to their symbolic character; rather almost always finished pictures were taken from Egyptian, Greek, or Roman iconography, and familiar pictorial schemata that were probably considered "tried and tested" were adopted.'[25]

Starting from Egypt, magic gems were spread by all social strata of the Roman population, by soldiers and merchants, throughout the Roman Empire. However, as early as the third century AD, they were increasingly fought against and finally suppressed:

'With the steadily increasing power and supremacy of Christianity and the sharp legal measures of canonical law, magic fell deeper and deeper into condemnation. Initially the clerics were forbidden, under threat of excommunication. For those involved with witchcraft and similar crafts or the fabrication and wearing of amulets, in AD 357 Constantine instituted the death penalty by decapitation for performers of any form of magic and predictions of the future, even for people who only wore amulets for protection against sickness.'[26]

There is much to suggest that the repressive methods of the Christian leaders and imperial administration were only partially successful: the magical lithotherapy was deeply rooted in Late Antiquity medicine and had proved to be successful for doctors. This healing practice was so firmly established that in the seventh century AD, the encyclopaedist Isidore, Bishop of Seville, determined that it was a proven remedy for a number of afflictions. The gemstone book written by Hildegard von Bingen documented magical lithotherapy – like all the rest of the medieval gemstone books – as an effective recipe of Christian healing methods, especially when the effect of the stones were supported through prayer. With neo-Platonism in the Renaissance, the late ancient esotericism of Alexandrian Egypt was revitalised under the guise of alchemy. During this epoch not only were the first modern collections of ancient 'magic gems' created but also a large number of

25 Simone Michel (note 21), p. 7.

26 Ibid., p. 232.

modern falsifications which contributed to modern esotericism. It shows – one would almost be inclined to say, prototypically – in this a procedure that is practiced to the present day: in all cases it is not the material itself that is the basis of its effectiveness but a magic spell spoken over the stone. These magical formulas are those of ancient Egypt, those of the 'gemstone medicine' of Hildegard von Bingen and also in the form of a modern love spell, or exchange, through magical formulas such as ritual dedications, prayers or verification processes through certificates of authenticity.

Gemstones as official seal and political index: Varieties of stone already used in the production of large quantities of everyday items were also used in the manufacture of seals and magical gems. While in the case of the magic gems the assignment of meaning takes place by an act of consecration, in the case of the Greek seals this is established as a means by law to secure against falsification.[27] Nevertheless it seems that there were rights of privilege which assigned certain minerals to the sphere of the divine, thus prohibiting a profane use. In the sphere of the holy, the religious or political leaders as well as the Israelite high priests or the Pharaohs were included. Thus Pliny reports in the first pages of his *Naturalis Historiae Liber XXXVII* [Natural History XXXVII] on several myths in which a luxurious abuse of precious stones is punished by the gods.[28] He notes that since the victory of Pompey over Mithridates (King of Pontus) in 1 BC, the use of gemstones and pearls as fashion had become popular in Rome, and he criticises this luxury with harsh words.[29] Pliny stood with this critical viewpoint in a long Roman tradition: the Lex Oppia of 215 BC, for example, forbade women to wear certain clothing and jewellery.[30] Even in Late Roman Antiquity, which was already influenced by Christianity, there were critical voices against the monetary valuation of gemstones, such as that of the philosopher Anicius Manlius Boethius (ca. AD 476–524).[31]

---

27 According to Diogenes Laertius in the sixth century BC, a statute was enacted within Solonistic Law stating that it was illegal for the stone carvers to duplicate a seal. See also Peter Zazoff, *Die antiken Gemmen: Handbuch der Archäologie*, Munich, 1983, p. 99.

28 C. Plinius Secundus (note 12), pp. 17 ff.

29 Ibid., pp. 23 ff.

30 See Elena Esposito, *Die Verbindlichkeit der Vorübergehenden: Paradoxien der Mode*, Frankfurt/Main, 2004, p. 20.

31 Anicius Manlius Boethius, *Trost der Philosophie*, Frankfurt/Main and Leipzig, 1997, pp. 83 and 87.

It is known that the morally justified condemnation could not successfully stop either the profanation of the gemstone or the luxury item being worn in public. With the expansion of the Roman Empire towards the East in the first to third centuries AD, it became increasingly fashionable among wealthy community members to trim clothing, shoes, harnesses and saddles of horses with gemstones.[32] Borne on old (imperial) rights, which reserved the wearing of certain purple fabrics and gemstones for imperial representation, Emperor Leo I (457–474) introduced a comprehensive legal regulation on imperial reservation rights with regard to gemstones.

'The Emperor Justinian: No one shall hereafter be permitted to decorate the bridles and saddles of his horses, or his own belts with pearls, emeralds, or hyacinths, or to insert them therein. We, however, permit them to adorn the bridles and saddles of their horses, and their own belts with other jewels. We order that, hereafter, all jewels of every description shall be removed from clothing, and that buckles which are valuable only for the gold of which they are composed, and their workmanship, shall be used on military cloaks. Moreover, if anyone should violate this law, he is hereby notified that he will immediately be fined fifty pounds of gold. Again, no private person shall be permitted to make anything out of gold and jewels, which is reserved for Imperial use and adornment (with the exception of ornaments usually worn by women, and the rings of both sexes), and no one shall be allowed to manufacture anything of this kind under the color or pretext of making a present of the same to the Emperor, for he does not expect it, nor does the reverence due to royalty require such donations by private individuals. If anyone should, hereafter, violate any of the provisions of this law, and be so bold as to fabricate any ornaments decorated with gold and jewels which are exclusively destined for the use of the Emperor, with a view to their being offered to him, he is hereby notified that he will be sentenced to pay a fine of a hundred pounds of gold, and also suffer capital punishment. Imperial ornaments must be made in the palace, by the artificers attached to the same, and not indiscriminately in private residences or workshops. Therefore, We order that this offence shall be punished with exemplary severity, in order that private persons may not rashly venture to make what is solely

32 See Gerda Friess, *Edelsteine im Mittelalter: Wandel und Kontinuität in ihrer Bedeutung durch zwölf Jahrhunderte (In Aberglauben, Medizin, Theologie und Goldschmiedekunst)*, Hildesheim, 1980, p. 60.

reserved for the splendor and adornment of the sovereign. If anyone should commit an act in violation of this law, We order that the fine above mentioned shall be collected by the officers of the palace, and paid into the Treasury of the Imperial Largesses.' [33]

From political symbol to religious cult practices: Between the first century BC and the sixth century AD, gemstones went through a process of change from a sacral to a governmental national emblem, accompanied by decisive moral criticism. This criticism changes simultaneously from an outrageous desecration of the divinity of blessed stones to a condemnation of luxury that calls forth the jealousy of the Gods. The transition to a governmental national emblem takes place more easily against the background of a God-given empire.

Similarly there are historically substantiated relations between the religious and political symbolism of gemstones. On the one hand they are attributed to the antique religions (Judaism, Christianity) or the sphere of godly mythologies. On the other hand were the imperial reservation rights, limiting the wearing of certain stones to the imperial family, which emerged in the Late Antiquity Byzantine era (fifth century AD). Thereby the gemstone receives an indexical function of a certain social status (insignia of rank).

Gerda Friess has shown that in the Early Middle Ages (Frankish Emperor era), a transfer of Byzantine practices into Western European political symbolism and also into Christian symbolism and Christian rituals took place: gemstones are particularly sanctified as reliquaries and in religious rites (crucifixes, chalices, etc.). In this context the ancient Pharaohs and Caesars are gods, and the German Kaisers are sovereigns of the Holy Roman Empire and are empowered through a religious iconic act.[34] Particularly noteworthy is that the transfer of imperial reservation rights to Christ begins almost simultaneously with the formulation of these rights in the Constantine era:

'In the time after Constantine the Great, the Christianisation of the empire led to a transfer of the three or four gemstones that had become a sign of monarchical representation to Christ. According to neo-Platonic thought processes, the perception was that the emperor

---

33 See The Codex of Justinian XXII, XI, 12, 1, available at: https://droitromain.univ-grenoble-alpes.fr/Anglica/CJ11_Scott.gr.html#11:

34 See Gerda Friess (note 32), pp. 64–74.

is an emanation of God. Because the sovereign acted, governed and lived through Christ, the King of Kings, his reservations and insignias became those of Christ. The expression of this mentality is apparent in the mosaics and frescoes. At this point ruby, emerald, sapphire and pearl, the representatives of the Late Antiquity and early Byzantine emperors' monarchical sublimity, also come into use as designations of the Kingdom of Christ. Gemstone-encrusted thrones, surely initiated through actual imperial archetypes, were prepared for Christ; the reserved stones adorn cruciform halos, chalices, and gospel books. Mary, the offspring of the royal house of David, wears royal gemstone-studded raiment and a tiara.'[35]

Christianity supports the transfer of imperial reservations through recourse upon the Old Testament's assignment of gemstones to God and the cult of God and upon the New Testament's revelation of John, in which 'Heavenly Jerusalem' is built upon gemstones. In this respect Christianity in the Early Middle Ages resumed the ancient cult including the sanctification of precious stones. A rich Christian gemstone allegory developed in parallel from late Antiquity to the Middle Ages. Gemstones refer to numerous Old and New Testament sources with references or symbolic characters in relation to the deity, at the same time directly accruing miraculous powers from them.[36] These ideas not only fulfilled popular beliefs but were also cultivated in the High Middle Ages, especially by mystical philosophers such as Bonaventura. Through the reassignment of gemstones to the sphere of the saint, which were made visible to the public through their use in sacred instruments such as chalices, monstrances, crucifixes, tabernacles, etc., gemstones have a symbolic charge that far exceeded the effect of reservation rights. This symbolic charge is still effective today.

The Catholic Church of Late Antiquity and the Middle Ages is, without a doubt, more than aware of the political function of gemstones in church services, although this has, thus far, received little scientific consideration – especially because during the Middle Ages it led a long acrimonious, smouldering conflict, enforcing

35 Ibid., p. 64.

36 Shedding light upon this theme at this point would burst the objective target and framework of this essay. This subject received in-depth scientific research by Christel Meier in Gemma Spiritalis: *Methode und Gebrauch der Edelsteinallegorese vom frühen Christentum bis ins 18. Jahrhundert*, part 1, Munich, 1977. The author unfortunately has not yet released part 2. An interesting archaeological paper is also Wolfgang Zwickel (ed.), *Edelsteine in der Bibel*, Mainz, 2002.

imperial investiture through the Pope. Sovereign gemstones were cultivated as symbols of triumphant Christianity. The advent of gemstone symbolism by Abbot Suger of St. Denis (1081–1151) is, in my opinion, to be understood and also evaluated from a political standpoint. Since the monastery near Paris is the burial place for French kings, it has considerable political meaning. An Abbot for many years, he established the generous usage of gemstones in the expansion of the cathedral of St. Denis, despite heavy criticism within the church from, among others, Bernard of Clairveaux.

'The life-giving cross, the salvific sign of the eternal victory of our salvific bearer, of whom the apostle says: But to me be far from being praised, unless in the name of the cross of my Lord Jesus Christ, is much more glorious, not only for men but all the more for angels, when the sign of the Son of Man appears to them in the highest heights in heaven; how much more glorious still – if it were in the trinkets, we could rely on it in the full worship of our Spirit, greeting it eternally with the Apostle Andrew: "Hail, Cross, consecrated by the body of Christ and adorned by its limbs as with pearls." Because we could not do as we actually wanted, the better we wanted to be able to do it, the more carefully we carried out (the work) for the all-giving God. Here is what wealth of precious pearls and precious stones we have requested everywhere ourselves or through our messengers; of which we have obtained as much as possible in the preparation of precious material of gold and precious stones for such a great jewellery; we have called together artists from all parts of the country who, with diligence and according to their own style, have worshipped the venerable cross with the admirable gems in the making of the sacrifice, and before them, apparently in the sight of the priest who made the sacrifice, have made a venerable image of our Lord, the Saviour, in remembrance of his suffering and suffering endured with such great patience.' [37]

In this multilayered process within the religious domain, gemstones are given three functions that work side by side: As a symbol of the worship of God, effectively in the tradition of Antiquity sacrifices, so to speak,

37 Suger, who Erwin Panofsky regarded – not unchallenged – as the style-forming patron of a Gothic cathedral, justified this with reference to Paul, Letter to the Galatians VI, 14, in '*Sugerii abbatis sancti Dionysii liber de rebus in administratione sua gestis*', in *Œuvres complètes*, ed. A. Lecoy de la Marche, Paris, 1867, p. 194.

- as a part of the sphere of the holy, they become holy themselves, and
- as magical objects connected with interceding prayers.

The gemstone as an object of Middle Ages science: There were varying handcraft practices well into modern times; however, there was very little progress based upon insight, in relation to Antique knowledge in the natural philosophical sciences. This according to Otto Mazal: 'The attempts at ordering minerals according to general factors without the exact knowledge of the chemical and physical characteristics of the minerals must remain incomplete, since only the criteria available are external data such as solidity, softness, colour, ability to smelt and similar data.'[38] This author is only able to detect true natural scientific progress from the seventeenth century on.[39]

In the Middle Ages one usually refers to ancient sources like Theophrast and Pliny, but also adopts, like Albertus Magnus, Arab authors like Ibn Sina (Avicenna). With the increasing cultural exchange with the Islamic world from the eleventh/twelfth century onwards, the reception of alchemical authors began. The origin of this tradition is mostly to be found in the legendary – already quoted by Albertus Magnus – Hermes Trismegistos in Alexandrian Late Antiquity. Apparently, however, there may have been other sources like the 'Lauteren Brueder', a Sufis secret society based in Basra around AD 950, which gained considerable influence upon later European alchemy.[40]

Medieval literature is – with one notable exception – either encyclopaedic[41] or 'medically' magical. In Europe at that time, there were over a hundred gemstone books that dealt with medicinal effectuality.[42] While the authors of Antiquity – for instance Theophrast or Pliny – had a certain inductive feedback to contemporary natural philosophy, this was almost entirely lacking during

38 Otto Mazal, *Geschichte der abendländischen Wissenschaft des Mittelalters*, vol. 2, Graz, 2006, p. 214.

39 Ibid., p. 219.

40 See Gernot Böhme and Hartmut Böhme, *Feuer, Wasser, Erde, Luft: Eine Kulturgeschichte der Elemente*, Munich, 2014, pp. 122–6. According to his doctrine, mercury and sulphur as intermediary chemical substances between the elements are involved in the formation of minerals.

41 The first medieval encyclopaedist is Isidore of Seville (seventh century).

42 See Müller 1984 (note 16). See also Meier 1977 (note 36).

the Middle Ages. The exception is Albertus Magnus with *De Mineralibus*. Of this comprehensive work only the chapter dealing with the magical-medical effects of stones was translated into German. In his first book of *De Mineralibus*, Albertus Magnus fundamentally categorises mineralogy into Aristotelian physics, which to date has unfortunately not been adopted and deserves greater interest, particularly in scientific history.

Therefore until the end of the Middle Ages, one cannot speak of a material science of gemstones. However, there are popular 'theories' about the emergence of gemstones and their impact, some of which have lasted into the early Modern Era. On this the following three examples:

- Pliny reports on the rock crystal: it originates in the icy heights of the highest mountains through the conjuncture of water and the sun's glow. Behind this idea is Aristotelian teaching, according to which elements, under certain circumstances, are substantially transformed: in the dry heights the power of the sun extracts the moisture from the frozen water so that the frozen water changes through transubstantiation into a crystal, all the while retaining its transparency.[43]
- Theophilus Presbyter, d. 1125. The diamond (adamas = indestructible) can only be worked if it had lain in the still warm blood under the heart of a freshly slaughtered buck in order for it to soften. This is a reversal of an analogy according to which the hardest, purest and most beautiful material can only be worked on by combining it with the liveliest, softest part of the ugliest creature. An idea that has been handed down since Antiquity, when none of the authors of that time had ever seen a diamond. *'If, however, you wish to cut the crystal, take a two- or three-year-old goat, tie its legs together, cut a hole between the chest and stomach at the location of the heart and place a crystal inside, so that it lies in its blood until it is warm. Remove the crystal and cut it, however you wish, as long as it is still warm, and if it begins to cool and harden, return it to the goat's blood,*
- *and once it is warm, remove it and continue to cut it, and continue in this manner until you have completed the relief.'*[44]

43 Magnus 1967 (note 14), Tractate 1.

44 Theophilus Presbyter, 'De Diversis Artibus', in Erhard Brepohl, *Theophilus Presbyter und das mittelalterliche Kunsthandwerk*, Cologne, Weimar and Vienna, 2013, p. 496.

- The dark red glimmering stones (carbuncles – carbunculi: rubies and garnets) are, according to Christian medieval preconception, the holiest and most valuable, because the light radiating out of the darkness most aptly represents godly strength. In the medieval metaphor of light, light refers to the deity.
  'Carbunculus, which is anthrax in Greek, and is called rubinus (ruby) by some, is a stone that is extremely clear, red and hard. It is to other stones as gold is to the other metals. It is said to have more powers than all other stones, as we have already said. But its special effect is to disperse poison or vapour in the air. When it is really good, it shines in the dark like a live coal, and I myself have seen such a one. But when it is less good, though genuine, it shines in the dark as if clear limpid water has been poured over it in a clean, polished black vessel.' In the fifteenth century this concept was still pervasive; according to Michael Baumann in his 'book of nature', he states on sicknesses and other things: 'The other question is how the powers get into the stone. So that they are good against some diseases and other things. The answer is: from where should the stone have the strength, other than from God, that is known to men. Sinners, it is certain that all power comes from God, as the holy teachers speak. But in the herbs and fruits, the powers are the effect of nature, that is the things that are hot or cold and good for medicine. And there are none of these things in any stone, as great heat or great cold is not tested in any stone, and so it has been revealed that in the medium of God, the Lord has given the stone the power of his grace for nature and thus the power of atonement.' [45]

Gemstones as luxury items: essentially 'gemstones' are not yet objects that are perceived aesthetically (sensually). They are as such not yet art objects in a modern sense. Especially in Antique Roman Literature and in Late Antiquity/Early Middle Ages and in connection with the handling of 'gems', there exists a condemnation of their profane usage as 'luxuria' (luxury items) – which is, however, generally not perceived in present-day literature. Thus

45 See Magnus 1967 (note 14), Tractate II, Chap. III: Klara Berzeviczy (ed.), *Michael Baumanns Naturbuch. Abdruck der Unikathandschrift und Begleitstudie*, Berlin, 2011, p. 165.

the 'murrhine vessels' made of precious minerals, of which Pliny speaks, are desecrated cult objects which are sacrilegiously used for luxurious purposes. (Pliny connects thereby the myth of The Ring of Croesus with the myth of Prometheus.)

In the Middle Ages the 'ennoblement' of the gemstones takes place through religious or political reservation rights, which reserve them for the spheres of the godly or lordly. The proximity to these spheres elevates them to the attribute 'precious'. As a part of Creation, gemstones are part of God's works. The 'virtute' (powers) of gemstones are an expression of godly effect. Further meaning is expressed through analogy – for example, through healing by touch with the holy rites or assignment to a certain sphere ('Heavenly Jerusalem').

In the epoch lasting until the High Middle Ages, there were two parallel practices of working gemstones: muggling and lapidary cutting. The latter became a skill in the production of sacred objects. This remarkable skill of the gem cutter, for which I would like to introduce the Greek term technê, stands in stark contradiction to the grinding of stones, which was more like a manual rubbing and polishing. In lapidary cutting there were already highly developed techniques for the engraving and drilling of gemstones.

The Modern Age turning point

During the middle of the thirteenth century, everything concerning gemstones began to change.
They became:

- profane, were treated as aesthetic objects and were manufactured accordingly (objects of profane beauty),
- a tradable commodity and
- objects of scientific study.

These aspects were developed simultaneously; the above order does not relate to their chronological appearance. At this time geology in the modern sense had not yet been developed, or for that matter crystallography – that would not see the light until well into the nineteenth century. In connection with the medieval mining industry, mineralogy and some areas of chemistry – as an ore-separation science – had their beginnings in metallurgy. Alhazen's already advanced Arabic optics was almost never adopted and remained ineffective. The five phenomena of change are:

1. Middle Ages: Stones were faceted (middle of the thirteenth century). The previous inner light was discovered to be cut creating a light effect (from glow to brilliance [Ger.: *brillieren*, Fr.: *briller*]).
2. Early Renaissance: Beginning of a reception, based on a formal language that touched on geometry, of Vitruv and the Euclidean theory of proportion.
3. High Renaissance and humanism: Plato was popularised through neo-Platonism – especially by Nicolaus Cusanus, Marsilio Ficino, and Giordano Bruno in Florence, and also in many parts of Europe – and reinterpreted in the spirit of the epoch. The geometric form is interpreted metaphysically.
4. Baroque: The perfect form of the round-cut brilliant, being in fact a primordial form of our brilliant-cut and in its literal expression connected to the French *briller*, was developed and becomes the expression of godly beauty and wisdom, and also the transmittal of this – that is, out of the human sphere.
5. The modern definition for mineralogy begins in humanism. Georgius Agricola (1494–1555), however, addresses mountain ore mining and pyrometallurgy. The discovery of gemstones was, if anything, a side effect of mountain ore mining that has hardly any relevant economic bearing. This does not change until the sixteenth century through the advent of global overseas trade shipping.

Conclusion: Gemstones became profane jewellery objects – and tradable goods – in the rationalistic age of mercantilism at the European courts.

The pre-industrial prototyping of the ideal cut

In the thirteenth century the faceting of (jewellery) stones began along with an astonishing turning point in Europe in the processing of minerals. More precisely: the change in the processing procedure was a symptom of a cultural upheaval. This expressed itself especially through a new relationship to nature. The medieval system of analogies, built upon the kinship of essentialities, began to waver. The form – or in other words, the sensually perceptible surface of objects – gained importance. Faceting and taste development were temporally subordinate phenomena. Technically it was, of course, possible to cut facets prior to this time, as gemstone cutting shows; however, no one saw any reason for it. In the Middle

Ages assigning meaning to precious stones took place on the basis of analogies which accorded the material a closer proximity or connection to God, to the sacred, to secular rule (before God's grace). In this respect the outer form was secondary.

While gemstone cutting in Antiquity and the Early Middle Ages led to remarkable craftsmanship, including sophisticated surface treatment and drilling techniques, the grinding sector was also marked by considerable technical backwardness.

Gustav Edmund Pazaurek summarises Middle Ages gemstone grinding as follows: 'Gemstone processing in the Occident was at a very primitive level during the Carolingian, Ottoman or Stauffer periods. The more valuable the stones, the smaller the pieces that were available, and these were nearly exclusively muggled, which means using your hands without devices and abrading upon a hard stone surface with water and sand until the desired shape, often still somewhat irregular, was achieved. Then, in order to achieve a highly reflective surface, it was polished upon lead plates and wooden discs, ultimately with stretched stag leather, both with fine, wet brick, also with saliva (!). Aside from this sleek finishing process, two other, even more cumbersome and time-consuming processes were known specifically for large crystal objects, namely drilling through and sawing.'[46] The author places the first substantiated use of manually driven grinding mills in the thirteenth century, where the gemstone workers procured them from the blacksmiths or weaponsmiths, who had already been using this method for some time for polishing metals.

Alf Schroeder, who places the first use of water-driven grinding mills in the thirteenth century at a Solingen sword and dagger manufacturer, dates the first verification of the use of gemstone-grinding machinery during the Hussite wars around 1430. Schroeder provides detailed evidence of the evolution of grinding technology between the fifteenth and eighteenth centuries, which refers not only to the energy source (water, horse or human power) but above all also to transmission. The main development is the horizontally rotating grinding wheel, whose speed is increased by the largest possible transmission wheels in order to be able to grind hard stones such as diamonds.[47]

---

46 Gustav E. Pazaurek, *Mittelalterlicher Edelsteinschliff*, Vienna, Leipzig and Zurich, 1930, p. 9.

47 Alf Schroeder, *Entwicklung der Schleiftechnik bis zur Mitte des 19. Jahrhunderts*, dissertation, 1930, Hoya, 1931, pp. 28 ff.: 'Admittedly very little can be gleaned from

Water-power-driven grinding mills existed in the region around Freiburg around the middle of the fifteenth century. In the time frame documented by Pazaurek, the grinding of smaller stones became an increasingly common practice. The faceting of stones was not induced by the invention of the grinding wheel; rather the adoption of the tried and tested gemstone-grinding techniques allowed the implementation of facet cutting in the mass production of gemstones. The new technology ultimately fostered the emergence of a phenomenal fashion during the Baroque era – in this case, the wearing of faceted gemstones. This, via Paris,[48] established the profane use of gemstones as an ornamental apparel element and increasingly began to supplant conventional gemstone grinding. The operative application of a machine allows the assertion of a normative form. To date, secured through analogies, the symbolic potency of stones – the inner worth of the substance (the godly light), the immediate proximity to holy objects in sacral rituals, and biblical legends about holy Jerusalem built upon gemstones – wanders into the outer form and becomes an object of aesthetic contemplation. Whereas the grinding machines considerably eased the faceting of smaller stones and thereby enabled their mass distribution, the reflective effect of the facet evoked their distribution as fashion. Thus the technical product 'facet' – a technem that bears witness to its technical-industrial production – becomes a prerequisite for an early fashion trend.

A central and, strangely, mostly overlooked effect of this process is that with the new processing technique a very much functionalistic handling of the material prevailed, which ultimately

---

the preceding information concerning how the gemstone grinding mills functioned, according to a medieval swordsmith. It was not until a manuscript (codex Latin no. 197, p. 23, reverse side) on the Hussite wars (ca. 1430), in which a Venetian gemstone grinding machine is depicted, was found in the Bavarian State Library in Munich. An explanatory notation completes the sketch: "*Item daz ist ein polier muss als dy hochn maister tzu Venedig haben darauff man allerley gestain poliert dy bedarf III scheiben dy erst in pleyen dy ander zynen dy tritt kupffern*" (as a high master in Venice, a polisher needs an object on which all kinds of stones can be polished; you will need three different discs, the first of lead, the second of tin, the third of copper).'

48 Ernest Babelon reports in his *Histoire de la gravure sur gemmes en France*, Paris, 1902, p. 151, that in the middle of the seventeenth century, there were no gemstone engravers to be found in Paris, because the art of gemstone engraving had been completely displaced by the trend of faceting gemstones, forcing Ludwig XIV to send a gemstone engraver to Florence as an apprentice, since he wanted to be independent of the imported cameos from other countries, particularly from Northern Italy. His book also documents to what degree France had profited, and would continue to profit, from the presence of Northern Italian gemstone engravers.

led to a change in meaning. Whereas the medieval belief that a substantial expression of God's will was demonstrated through the shining light emanating from the darkness of the carbuncle stone, the light effect of brilliance now became the object of representation. The object, more or less left in its natural state, became an artefact with a different meaning. The material disappeared, as it were, behind its image and ultimately in the effect of the brilliant light.

Even before the Industrial Revolution, the prototype of the gemstone was created in this way, which finally shaped our present ideas of the gemstone but also our ideas of the natural mineral. The artefact became the model for reality. I myself have, during my years of teaching, asked students to spontaneously draw gemstones – with the result that about ninety per cent of the drawings depicted the schematic outer form of a brilliant-cut diamond from above or in profile.

I would like to mention again the Greek term technê for the process of producing the prototype of the 'gemstone' as described above – aware that it will collide with today's term 'technique'. Technê meant, at a former time, the whole of all relationships of science and practice: from cosmology to knowledge of material, and the study of proportion, the proficient knowledge of tools and processing methodology. In this respect, art/technê still means the content-related linking of processing technology and world view. However, over the course of time, it experienced a conversion into today's term 'technology' and the concept of 'art' was largely eliminated from technê.[49]

The refinement of ever more differentiated facet-cutting shapes, established in the Renaissance, only apparently contradicts the humanistic gemstone symbolism fed by neo-Platonism. As the result of a rationalistic (machine) production process, the symbol of divine wisdom also becomes the symbol of human reason (ratio). However, this is contradicted by the optical tantalising sparkle effect on the eye achieved by the cut. This is increasingly the desired effect of the faceting. The light effect replaces the meaning of the material and causes the symbolic emptying of the meaning of the stone as material. The coruscation of the gemstone, caused by the faceting, is then reduced to a sensational effect, whose main purpose is to arouse the attention of the observer. The separation

---

49 This process was a subject of an earlier *ThinkingJewellery* symposium.

of elements of clothing from traditional contexts of meaning[50] and at the same time an effective but empty presentation are prerequisites for the fashion emerging in the Baroque period.

'In consideration of the complex situation, it may be useful to look at the tendencies and effectiveness of laws against the waste that has existed in one form or another, that has only been precisely normed, differentiated and brought forth between the various states. The attempt to regulate clothing and jewellery, indeed to control the world of the illusory, appears to have been important, especially in the period from the thirteenth to the sixteenth century – a time in which semantics were still attached to the Middle Ages' world view, a global order that regulated the entire cosmos, to the smallest detail, so that any manipulation of the illusory world was simultaneously perceived as an attack against this order and its legitimacy and had to therefore be sanctioned. This need for regulation apparently appeared the very moment this superimposed order began to falter, and it is especially the ambiguity of the laws against waste that also mirrors the ambiguity of this situation. The applicable provisions formulate specific, detailed prohibitions for all levels of society and confirm the hierarchical order and the attached prerogatives. Meanwhile the laws in the previous periods were only applicable to the lower levels of society and only appeared in the form of prohibitions; after the sixteenth century they implicitly

---

50 Concerning the Middle Ages' regulation of clothing, see Jean Baudrillard, *Symbolic Exchange and Death*, trans. Iain Hamilton Grant, London, 1993, pp. 71–2: *'The counterfeit (and, simultaneously, fashion) is born with the Renaissance, with the destruction of the feudal order by the bourgeois order and the emergence of overt competition at the level of signs of distinction. There is no fashion in a caste society, nor in a society based on rank, since assignation is absolute and there is no class mobility. Signs are protected by a prohibition which ensures their total clarity and confers an unequivocal status on each. Counterfeit is not possible in the ceremonial, unless in the form of black magic and sacrilege, which is precisely what makes the mixing of signs punishable as a serious offence against the very order of things. If we take to dreaming once more – particularly today – of a world where signs are certain, of a strong 'symbolic' order, let's be under no illusions. For this order has existed, and it was a brutal hierarchy, since the sign's transparency is indissociably also its cruelty. In feudal or archaic caste societies, in cruel societies, signs are limited in number and their circulation is restricted. Each retains its full value as a prohibition, and each carries with it a reciprocal obligation between castes, clans or persons, so signs are not arbitrary. The arbitrariness of the sign begins when, instead of bonding two persons in an inescapable reciprocity, the signifier starts to refer to a disenchanted universe of the signified, the common denominator of the real world, towards which no-one any longer has the least obligation.'*

allowed everyone access to jewellery and select clothing and only limited themselves in their distinction according to what class they belonged.'

Concerning the development of taste and the 'conversation myth' in the Baroque Age, see ibid., pp. 130–2: *'In this situation, regarding the lack of unified criteria, we make use of the "criteria without criterion" of good taste. [...] Taste thus enters into honnête. The honnête homme has good taste, and in order to recognise good taste, one must rely on the opinion of the honnête homme, who is refined through practice in conversation. The good taste becomes an indicator, which allows the reflective constitution of the identity of the individuals from arbitrariness and, at the same time, subscribes to and keeps the order of stratification. Everyone constitutes their own identity in the empty interaction and through the observation of being observed; there are nevertheless criteria that allow the ensuing results and orientate their own behaviour accordingly, regardless of how unutterable the good taste is uniformly recognised and can function as pseudo-criteria.'* [51]

The de-contextualisation, the eradication of the previous symbolic content, enables the transformation to a commodity that can be exchanged for other equivalents, especially money. Holy objects can actually only be used according to their ritual dedication. Their theft is illegal; their trade is more than despicable. The stone cut in this way, however, is not a completely arbitrary sign, since it is fitted into a general cultural context by the geometric language of forms in the sense of the classical theory of proportions. Furthermore it carries as an inherited liability the excellent classification 'precious'. The object becomes open for new meaning. As Epítheton órnans, ornamental decoration's entire function is to draw attention to the wearer. This is now modern or 'en vogue'.

The tantalising effect of the eye consists of the illusionistic orchestration of light living within the stone, which actually is generated by the external movement of the light source of the object or the observer. The illusionistic effect takes the place of symbolism. The emptying of meaningful content allows its transformation into a fashionable accessory for clothing and thus fulfils an important requirement for its popularisation.

---

51 The transition from the medieval 'clothing order' to Baroque fashion is gradually consummated between the thirteenth and sixteenth centuries. Concerning the emergence of fashion of the Baroque Age, see Esposito 2007 [note 30], pp. 20 ff.

Geometric form and cosmological interpretation

The canonisation process of gemstone cutting begins in the second half of the fourteenth century.[52] By the seventeenth century a series of cut types was developed, which in the nineteenth and twentieth centuries were equipped with a binding set of rules by the newly developed gemology. Between the Renaissance and Baroque, the basic cut forms for the table cut and the brilliant cut evolved. They followed the fundamental taste ideals of this epoch in the form of geometric principles. Essential achievements of Renaissance art in the course of a general return to Antiquity were the rediscovery of Vitruvius (born between 80 and 70 BC) and finally the Euclidean theory of proportions. Art and architecture of the Renaissance developed the concept of an ideal beauty, which followed the rules of beauty in nature laid down by God. God, who is believed to be a rational being, created the world according to a geometric set of rules – de more geometrico.

Anselmus de Boodt, the author of the first comprehensive handbook on modern gemstone science, conveyed the following instructions for the cutting of table-cut diamonds: '*The diamond is cut into a form in varying ways. Wherein the preferred shape is a basic square (basal) shape. This is accomplished by forming the upper side into a square surface. If, however, the diamond is to be shaped in this way, it must be ensured that two (opposite) lateral surfaces form an upper surface and that the lateral angles form the hypotenuse at right angles. Then it is so. Ultimately it is necessary that one top portion has a longer (larger) table than the other. In this manner the form is the most perfect. If it is made of pure substance in which no colour appears, its price is usually estimated at 5 ducats if it weighs one ceratium. [...] There will be a remainder of raw pyramid-shaped diamonds, as they (by nature) are a derivative of the square. Although this form is occasionally preferred, in comparison to others it is still less dignified and valuable than the table form. Other cuts, due to the (natural) shape of the stones, are selected in order to minimise loss to the body.*'[53]

---

52 See Fritz Falk, *Edelsteinschliff und Fassungsformen im späten Mittelalter und im 16. Jahrhundert*, Ulm, 1975, pp. 15 ff.; Herbert Tillander, *Diamond Cuts in Historic Jewellery 1381–1910*, London, 1995, p. 25; Wilhelm Lindemann, 'From Iconic Gemstone to Contemporary Art Object', in W. Lindemann (ed.), *Edelstein/Kunst: Rennaisance bis heute. Gemstone/Art: Renaissance to the Present Day*, Stuttgart, 2016, pp. 66–126.

53 Anselmus de Boodt, *Gemmarum et Lapidarum Historia*, Leyden, 1648, Chap. VII, p. 139. The term *ceratium* remains untranslated, since it does not conform to the current measurement unit carat. In this period one carat of gold was approximately equivalent to one gramme.

The transformation from the square to the round form takes place in several steps at the French courts of the fifteenth and sixteenth centuries. The twelve-facet round Burgundy cut was first developed into a taille en seize, composed of sixteen triangular facets, in order to achieve its ultimate form, the brilliant cut, at the end of the sixteenth century at the court of Louis XIV. Its round-cut shape combined the increasing number of facets with one large one, derived from the table cut as the crown.[54] Herbert Tillander apparently sees certain influences after the import of Indian diamonds worked in the 'Mughal-cut'[55] which Jean-Baptiste Tavernier (1605–1689) had brought to the French court from his travels to India between 1630 and 1675; moreover he sees, on the whole, a trend in the development of the cuts towards the brilliant effect.

That faceting became established as a processing practice for gemstones between 1350 and 1700 is primarily due to the aesthetic ideas of the Renaissance and Baroque epochs, in addition to the technological developments described above. There is no major influence from the findings of simultaneously emerging optics or even crystallography; Nicolaus Stenos's discovery of the law of angular constancy in crystals in 1669 had no consequences for the processing of gemstones. On the one hand the developing popularity of faceted gemstones at the French court was due to the fashion developments highlighted below. On the other hand in the outer shape of the stone as well as in the development of the facets, a geometric language of form revealed a vocabulary of symbols that had its roots in the neo-Platonic philosophy of the Renaissance and transitioned in the rationalistic era through a large number of humanistic academics and artists.[56]

In the age of humanism, at least in the relevant educated classes, the circle as the symbol of the divine Universal One and universal representation of the 5th, the cosmos forming element, and the triangle as the formative basis of the four Platonic elements earth, water, air and fire enjoy considerable popularity.

---

54 This development is portrayed in detail in Tillander 1995 (note 52).

55 Tillander 1995 (note 52), pp. 64–5. With the Mughal cut many irregular, lateral facets surround the crown facet. The East Indian cut is only known through its irregular, non-geometrical faceting, since faceting machines were not yet in use in the seventeenth century.

56 See Lindemann 2016 (note 52).

As a symbolic depiction of the variety of things unfolding from the godly principle of the One (circle), the brilliant stone especially stands for godly wisdom as well as human reason, which in neo-Platonic philosophy portrays the human as the soul spark of godly wisdom.

Indications of emerging doubts about the reality of the medieval world order are not only to be found in the artistic expressions of Mannerism; it is an ongoing occupation of philosophy, from Descartes to Kant, asking the question as to the recognisability of the world. This scientific theoretical discourse continues to this day.

Rationalism has not only, on the political side, legitimised the Absolutist State but also, in the era of mercantilism, theoretically substantiated the capitalistic exchange of goods. I would like to place the beginning of 'crystalline thinking' in this convergence of aesthetics, science, economics and politics.

On the other hand, for all the rationalistic interpretation of the brilliant cut, the brilliant trompe l'oeil effect shows a deep uncertainty: it is based upon a deception of the senses, which simulates a living, coruscating stone while in reality it is simply an effect produced by external motion. In the meaningless ornament – emptied of its purpose – the 'vanitas' motif and death appears.

Gemstones as commodities

This is a chapter that can only be touched upon as an aside, since in relation to the gemstone industry, only those aspects should be dealt with that directly deal with our field of expertise. However, a hint should be given: also mercantilism/early capitalism (sixteenth and seventeenth centuries) was a result of rationalist thinking – in relation to a nature 'subject' to man and in relation to the foundation of a rational organisation of economic life, in which the greatest possible benefit of the individual resulted in the greatest possible benefit for all. The market-based exchange of goods became the engine of social progress.

With the emergence of the mercantilist (early capitalist) trading system and the conquest of the world by the European powers, selected minerals (gold, silver, precious stones) became merchandise. Like all tradable objects, exchange for equivalent money took place, which must be measured in some form. Money thus became the symbolic equivalent of gemstones. Although the absolutist rulers of the Austro-German, French and English dynasties paid the bills, it was the people of Latin America or the slaves exported from Africa, and also their own people who paid the actual price of the 'luxuria'.[57]

From an economic perspective, the introduction of the faceting wheel, i.e. a machine for the production of facets, resulted in a considerable acceleration of the production process, which allowed the production of faceted stone beads at a much lower cost. The faceting wheel and, later, the faceting disc were technical necessities for serial production. The new technology was one of the prerequisites for the expansion of the gemstone industry – with foreseeable results.

Ernest Babelon reports in his *Histoire de la gravure sur gemmes en France*[58] that in the middle of the seventeenth century there were no more gemstone engravers in Paris, since the art of stone engraving had been completely suppressed by the fashion of cutting faceted gemstones. Thus Louis XIV was forced to send an engraver to Florence for training, since he wanted to make himself

---

57 The following is an example of dramatic criticism during the Classicistic era, delivered by Friedrich Schiller, *Plays: Intrigue and Love and Don Carlos*, ed. Walter Hinderer, New York, 2003, pp. 25–6.

'THE VALET: His Serene Highness the Duke recommends himself to my Lady's favor and sends these jewels for your wedding. They have just arrived from Venice.

LADY: (having opened the casket, falls back with fright): Man! What did your Duke pay for these stones?

VALET: (with a black look): They did not cost him a farthing.

LADY: What? Are you mad? Nothing? ... and (as she takes a step away from him you give me a look as if you would thrust a dagger through me ... These inestimably precious stones cost him nothing?

VALET: Yesterday seven thousand sons of the land left for America ... They pay for everything.

LADY: (suddenly puts the Jewellery down again and paces rapidly through the room; to the valet, after a pause): Man, what is the matter with you? I do believe you are weeping?

VALET: (wiping his eyes, in a fearful tone, trembling in every limb): Jewels like those ... I too have a couple of sons among them.

LADY: (turning away with a shudder and grasping his hand): But none taken by force?

VALET: (laughing horribly): Oh Lord ... No ... every one of them volunteers! A few saucy lads or so stepped up front and asked the Colonel how dear the sovereign was selling a yoke of human beings ... But our most gracious ruler had all regiments march out on the parade ground and had the loudmouths shot down. We heard the rifles crack, saw their brains splatter the pavement, and the whole army shouted: "Hurrah! Off to America!".'

(Friedrich Schiller, *Intrigue and Love II/2*. It pertains to the sale of soldiers, by the German princes, to the English, during the American War of Independence.)

58 Babelon 1902 (note 48), p. 151.

independent of the imports of cameos from abroad, primarily from Italy.

The rationalistic development of production technology corresponded to a relationship to nature that changed from the end of the Middle Ages onwards. Natural resources were no longer an expression of the gift of divine care and love; especially in the fifteenth and sixteenth centuries of the Reformation, they became the divine mission of controlling nature: subdue the earth. The facet cut also stood for this spiritual change.

For the customer commerce and 'money', as the equivalent in the exchange of goods, required comprehensible certification systems for the value of goods. For the gemstone market, too, a scientifically legitimate certification system, namely the certificate of authenticity and value of goods, was increasingly becoming the primary requirement. In the middle of the nineteenth century, the newly developed crystallography finally solved this problem.

Geometric symbolism was no longer adequate as a basis for assessment. There was a need for quantifiable, physical bases of assessment. Plainly stated, although the Middle Ages and early Modern Age analogies were passé, they were not altogether invalid. As a residue of the previous splendour, the term 'precious' and the perceived placement 'way up' in the hierarchy of things, close to the stars, was imbued with near supernatural powers – and with equivalent beauty.

The new analogies were those of exact natural sciences. Their peculiarity was that they converted the geometric assumptions about the outer world, which Descartes was still making, from expansion (extensio) into numerical forms of representation (length, weight, etc.). The carat[59] was introduced as a form of measurement,

---

59 The term *Karat* (carat) was already used in medieval metallurgy in Europe as a unit of weight for precious metals. At this time, however, they were not yet coordinated and indicated different sizes from country to country. See Georgius Agricola, *De re metallica Lib. XII*, Basel, 1556 (German trans.: Munich, 1977, p. 219): '*Die Münzleute, welche Goldmünzen schlagen, teilen die Mark ein in 24 binae sextulae, welche die Griechen ceratia nennen, die bina sextula in 4 semisextulae, die man Gran nennt, und die semisextulae in 3 quaternae siliquae, worunter wir Gränchen verstehen*' [The minters who mint gold coins divide the Mark into 24 *binae sextulae*, which the Greeks call *ceratia*, the *bina sextula* into 4 *semisextulae*, which is called *gran*, and the *semisextulae* into 3 *quaternae siliquae*, by which we mean grains]. The initial value for 1 Mark in the German realm represents, according to Agricola (ibid, p. 219), 233.856 grammes. Its equivalent is 24 *binae sextulae* (= *ceratia*/carat), or 96 *semisextulae grana* (1 *gran* = *scripula/scruples* = 288 *quaternae siliquae*).

the name of which derives from the seed kernel of the horn-shaped fruit of the carob tree, which in turn stems from the ancient Greek word keraton (small horn), the diminutive of keras, the ram's horn – at which point we arrive at the blood sacrifice of a ram (krios). To the 'C' of carat, the 'C's of colour, clarity and cut were later added. Thereby from the nineteenth century (metric conference of Brussels in 1875), the necessary symbolic certification system provided by the natural sciences was used when dealing with the authenticity and value of gemstones. In the nineteenth century, the field of gemology as an interest-driven special science segregated itself from mineralogy in order to determine and certificate the authenticity of gemstones.[60] With the rise of gemology, the basis for the subsequent assessment system was laid; this became a matter of urgency with the use of coloured glass stones in jewellery in the nineteenth century and the production of synthetic stones in the twentieth century.[61]

The profanation of gemstones reduced them to their commercial value. The trade thereof was, ultimately, a trade with certificates. The value of the certificate was determined by the brilliance of the stone. Gemstones became an object of avarice, a condition that Pliny as well as one of the Seven Deadly Sins already warned us about 2,000 years ago and in the Middle Ages.

---

60 See the following keyword: 'Gemmologie' at: https://de.wikipedia.org/wiki/Gemmologie. Gemology shall answer the following questions: a) The determination according to a mineralogical basis, b) The question regarding authenticity of the material, and c) Has it been treated? On the same Internet site is the self-portrayal of the German Gemmological Corporation in Idar-Oberstein.

61 See Joerg Staiber in the Nahe newspaper on 2 October 2017, p. 26: *'Trust is the most important capital. Gemstones in a trust crisis? […] This topic has a very serious and current background: the demand for high-quality coloured gemstones, but also for diamonds, has grown rapidly in recent years, with the Asian market playing a particularly important role. This demand cannot be satisfied as the deposits of coloured gemstones in particular are limited. This supply gap awakens desires and leads to unclean criminal practices, ranging from the false declaration of synthetic stones, via the manipulative transformation of inferior into higher quality gemstones, to a completely opaque certification practice. […] "In the past, the naturalness and beauty of a stone were the most important characteristics for the buyer," reported Constantin Wild. "Today it is what is written in sometimes questionable certificates. […] It is becoming increasingly difficult, even for experts, to distinguish a natural stone from a synthesis and to verify treatments to improve the quality of the stone." Even the most imaginative colour designations would now spread "like the plague", said Lind verbatim. This is also confirmed by Christian Klein for the diamond industry.'*

This was expressed in the transformation process in the standardisation of gemstone cuts in the seventeenth and eighteenth centuries to ideal-typical forms such as the brilliant cut. The industrially reproducible prototype of the gemstone was born. As a symbol of profane beauty, the formal design of the stone, which despite all contrary (scientifically proven) statements had nothing to do with the natural mineral, became an ornament or a decorative feature in the divertimento of courtly societies.

Even the face of Plato's 'godly demiurge', who at the end of his daily task decorated the heavenly cosmos with star-filled realms, has changed: in the conservative Biedermeier in the nineteenth century, it became the bookkeeper and a faithful, middle-class family man. Thus the Protestant priest and children's literature author Wilhelm Hey, in his nursery rhyme *Weißt du wie viel Sterne stehen?* [Do You Know How Many Stars There Are?], published in 1837, could write: '*Gott der Herr hat sie gezählet, dass ihm auch nicht eines fehlet an der großen Zahl*' [God the Lord has counted them, so that, out of the great number, not a single one is missing].

Counting in biblical language was a political, grand act that continued in the second verse in another act, namely the designation of plants and animals – in other words, categorisation or ordering for your enjoyment. The contrast to the Romantic concept, in which man was part of an altogether animated nature, is obvious: the delimiting nature poetry became the accounting transformation of nature, which was captured and represented in an arithmetic analogy: the convergence of science, art and pedagogy in a patriarchal bourgeois world.

In the early eighteenth century, the mineral, now transformed into a gemstone, found its ideal form with the prototypical shape of the round, faceted diamond, which has essentially been preserved and perfected to the present day with the teleological striving for perfect brilliance. It was the effort in achieving as perfect a reflection or collection of the light inside the stone as possible through faceting and radiating it in the direction of the observer. The goal was the transformation of the stone into light, its dematerialisation and elevation to a symbol, into which the buyer or owner could project anything he or she desired. In this form, the traditional gemstone has reached its ultimate goal. It is a place of solidification, where the mineral as a material becomes a dead stone. It even developed – especially in the association with greed and commerce after its transformation into exchangeable goods – into a mythical and literary symbol of misfortune and death. A gemstone curse existed that derived not from the stone itself but from greed, a form of crystalline thinking. Some believe that the diamond acquired thereby its fifth 'C': the crime. A characteristic of this 'crystalline thinking' could be the liaison of rationalistic-led trade and lack of ethical constraints.

The crystal on its way to the modern philosophy of nature

The initial situation: After this prehistory it was to be expected that gemstones, protected since Antiquity by reservation rights, would, with their increasing market dependency, irrevocably get lost in the sphere of commerce, luxurious lameness and boredom. In any case the increasing trade revenues were hardly used for stimulating the creativity of artists during the nineteenth and twentieth centuries. Therefore it is now time to carefully examine the next breathtaking turning point that the crystal has taken, first of all in the scientific thinking of the Modern Era, and then in art. The pioneering role of natural science must clearly be acknowledged here. Since the seventeenth century it has been working to liberate crystallisation from the sphere of inanimateness, at least as a testimony to past geological processes, and finally even to transfer it to the biosphere. Crystallisation became the structural formula of life in the morphology of Goethe and Romanticism. This is a scientific concept that is initially not counted among the players in the scene of the 'exact' natural sciences but has undoubtedly made a significant contribution to the foundation of modern natural sciences as well as the crystalline art symbol. In the following, several key witnesses shall support this thesis, although they themselves were frequently denied scientific credibility, since they had also become famous as artists.[62]

In the case of the crystal, considerable interactions of scientific and cultural-artistic interpretation and practical use (magical-religious, medical, economic, manual, etc.) can be observed in all eras of its use. Since Modern Age thinking also does not begin unconditionally in the somewhere of the sixteenth/seventeenth century, the relevant aspects of its prehistory cannot be completely ignored. Although Plato did not explicitly address the crystal or

62 Since the context of this essay is not the question of who has the truth on their side in the scientific argument but rather which position had influence, the theme can remain unattended in this paper.

crystallisation in his works, he should nevertheless be considered one of the intellectual forefathers of scientific theory and thus also of crystallography. Despite his crystal-like 'Platonic Bodies', he is not to be regarded as the inventor of crystallography, since he had no idea of crystals. For example, he considered the diamond to be an offshoot of gold.

In his work *Timaios*, Plato introduces his myth about the genesis of the world out of chaos. God, whom he called the great demiurge, was, in other words, a craftsman, since he was blessed with reason. He created a rational world according to a rational point of view and according to the principle of *kalokagathia* (the beautiful and good). First he created the elements water, fire, earth and air after rational factors. Taking the triangle as the smallest possible geometric form (of the surface), he introduced the four elements as tetrahedron (fire), octahedron (air), hexahedron or cuboidal (earth) and icosahedron (water). He also introduced the dodecahedron (ether), symbolising the cosmos that surrounds the earthly world, in the form of a hollow sphere. The Greek term denotes not only the twinkling universe but also ornaments (jewellery). 'He ornaments the ether' (Plato).

For the later history of the crystal, the following aspects from Plato's *Timaios* are noteworthy:

- He describes a myth, namely of the genesis of the world.
- The divine craftsman is a being of reason and creates a rational, i.e. well-ordered, world, because he cannot do anything other than what is beautiful and orderly.
- Only due to the fact that we humans carry a spark of the divine principle of reason within ourselves are we able to discern the world.

Plato is also not the inventor of geometry; others have worked on this rationalist project before him: first the Egyptians, then Pythagoras. The invention of geometry as one of the fundamental occurrences of human history[63] has cleared up the chaos of the world somewhat for humankind. The previously precipitous nothing (also the biblical Genesis calls it 'desolate and empty') became a geometrically dimensioned space and, in connection with arithmetic, even

63 On the historicity of geometry, see also Edmund Husserl, 'Der Ursprung der Geometrie', in Jacques Derrida, *Husserls Weg in die Geschichte am Leitfaden der Geometrie*, Munich, 1987.

calculable. This made a lot of things easier for mankind.[64] Geometry became a representation of the structural order of nature, especially also of the nature of crystals, whose inner structure unfolds geometrically. The basic presumption of the perceptibility of the world is based on the idea that nature and the perceptive human intellect (as a part of nature) operate according to the same logical organisational principle. It is the concept of the structural unity of the world and of the intellectual and the material – in other words, the unity of a rational order – that became the natural philosophical and epistemological basis of science and, therefore, our idea of what crystals are.

In this respect, the faceted cut stones of the Renaissance and Baroque periods convey above all the cosmological and natural philosophical concepts of these eras. Their shapes drew upon Platonism especially, at the height of the knowledge theory of the time; from there the faceted stones underwent a strong symbolic charge as rationalistic symbols of wisdom.[65]

Indeed the first doubts concerning the unity of the world and insight could have come up as early as the Renaissance: Florentine architects and artists realised that the geometric mathematically constructed space and the visually perceived empirical space are two different things, since the latter, from the (subjective) point of view of an observer, was perceived in perspective, towards the vanishing point. This is at least strange, if not a reason to doubt one's senses or the experience and truth of the world, in view of the fact that one can handle the world so practicably according to the mathematical-geometrical method of measuring space.

In the epoch of Rationalism – art historically we refer to it as Baroque – the modern 'exact' natural sciences agreed upon the application of the geometric-arithmetic process, namely the description and measurement of the world. Thus an autonomous scientific system emerged, which on the one hand was based on empiricism and is descriptive, and on the other hand, when it comes

64 Jacques Monod, *Chance and Necessity: An Essay on the Natural Philosophy of Modern Biology, trans. Austryn Wainhouse*, New York, 1972, p. 100: *'It may be asked, of course, whether all the invariants, conservations, and symmetries that make up the texture of scientific discourse are not fictions substituted for reality in order to obtain a workable image of it [...] accessible to the operations of a logic itself founded upon a purely abstract, perhaps "conventional" principle of identity – a convention which, however, human reason seems incapable of doing without.'*

65 See Wilhelm Lindemann in Lindemann 2016 (note 52), pp. 61–213.

to the formulation of laws of nature, had to adhere to the traditional method of contradiction-free deductive derivation. Objectivity of knowledge is achieved through experimentation, if the presentation of empirically won knowledge can be presented in a mathematically consistent manner. Since then there have been, aside from the analogue natural representation through graphics and numbers, never-ending attempts at applying systems of classification and order. Although this process is frequently criticised because of its inherent weaknesses, it is seldom called into question because of its practicability in contemporary natural sciences.[66] Rationalism, on the political side of things, has not only legitimised the absolutist nation but has also institutionalised capitalist commodity exchange with mercantilism.

It is at this convergence of aesthetics, science, economy and politics that I would like to situate the beginning of 'crystalline thinking'.

From Cosmology to Geology to Biology: The cosmological and natural philosophical content of the Pythagorean-Euclidian geometry in the natural sciences of the Modern Age is increasingly fading into oblivion. On the other hand, with René Descartes (1596–1650) and the fundamental demand for objectivity as a criterium for science, geometry and mathematics became the new leading sciences, not only for the natural sciences but also for philosophy, which for its part had been accepted as propaedeutic for the natural sciences. Even Leibnitz was a mathematician, and Kant began his scientific career with an astronomical work. Thus it is no wonder that the crystal-polyhedron would become the symbol for wisdom, science and scientific credibility.

The crystal-polyhedron is, however, more than just a symbol, at least in the work of Johannes Kepler (1571–1630), one of the most important protagonists of the 'Copernican Revolution' in the modern natural sciences. In his New Year's proclamation Strena: Of the Six-Sided Snow he writes:

---

66 Cartesianism introduces a scientific process of idealisation, of experimental exhaustion, of elementarism, of theoretical preformation of the phenomena to be recognised, which in its ahistoricity eliminates the recognising human being as well as the ethically acting being from objectivity. See Gernot Böhme, 'Ist Goethes Farbenlehre Wissenschaft?', in *Studia Leibnitiana IX*, no. 1, 1977, pp. 27–54; here: p. 45.

'Furthermore since it is completely certain that even the spirits in their innermost being accept quantities – whether without or with physical substance, I am not discussing – it is quite natural that they accept shaped rather than raw quantities, and if shaped, then according to the type of regular bodies, because it is not surfaces but bodies that are associated with the spirits. Of the regular bodies, the cube is the first, the first-born, the creator of the rest. His wife, however, is the octahedron; it has as many corners as the cube has surfaces, and each centre of these surfaces corresponds to one corner of the octahedron.

/ Thus a particle of the water vapour matter that separates – if it is to take shape, which we have already agreed on – seizes the figure of the cube and its companion, the octahedron, first. Which the material necessity above also suggested regarding a heap of equally sized spheres. They were thus combined and, at the points of contact, presented themselves as fragments of the cube and octahedron. For instance because the cube is the figure of expansion, the octahedron the figure of contraction? In reality, matter and thermal power contract when they are antagonistically threatened by the cold. Whence, however, is it certain that this is the figure of expansion, this the figure of contraction? Because the eight corners which sit on the very outside of it are arranged in equal numbers around the centre, of course. For if one takes away the eight corners of the cube by means of equally cut surfaces and assembles them inwards, an octahedron is created. And the cube divides into a larger number of corners, namely eight, and the octahedron into a smaller number, namely six.

/ The gemstone dealers say that diamonds have natural octahedrons of very perfect and very good limited form. If that's the case, it's very encouraging. For the ability to form, which gave the diamond the shape of an octahedron in the Earth, which comes from the deepest lap of nature at the same time as the water vapour, which comes from the same Earth, also lent the same figure to the snow, which is formed from that very vapour.'[67]

As Kepler wrote this New Year's greeting, he was working as an astrologer and astronomer at the court of Rudolf II, a European 'hotspot' of gemstone processing but also of alchemy. His comments on the formation of crystals pointed not only to alchemical, practical

67 Johannes Kepler, *Strena: Vom sechseckigen Schnee*, ed. W. Keiper, Berlin, 1948, pp. 28–9.

knowledge but also the practice of growing salt crystals from supersaturated brine practised since the Neolithic Age. The modern scientific occupation with gemstones also began at the imperial court of Rudolf II in Prague. From 1585 to 1612 Anselmus de Boodt (1550–1632), a physician, chemist and humanist from Bruges, was working in Prague as curator of the imperial gemstone collection. He wrote the first gemstone manual of the Modern Era, Gemmarum et Lapidarum Historia in 1609.[68] In the nearly 600-page work, he not only adopted the knowledge of gemstones from the entire Antiquity and Middle Ages periods but also delivered a detailed description of approximately 600 gemstones and listed a further 400 by name. His directory and description of gemstones was preceded by explanations of terms that mirrored the aesthetic and economic meaning of gemstones that evolved during the sixteenth century: great rarity, processing properties and natural beauty became the significant criteria.[69] With regard to the genesis of the stones, the Paracelsian brought the antique medieval views up to date at that time with a handbook for practising imperial collectors and, in particular, those who worked with gemstones, for whom there are many practical tips.

While de Boodt was aware that the focus was on the utilitarian aspects for the curator of the imperial collection, from the middle of the seventeenth century onwards representatives turned to the subject of modern natural sciences for the first time, with Nicolaus Stenson (Nicolaus Steno) (1638–1686) and Robert Boyle (1627–1691). While in medieval literature the (magical) properties of stones were described by the term 'virtues' (manliness, bravery, strength), now it was simply a matter of descriptive properties. Already with de Boodt the phenomenological description stood as starting point of the observation. Steno's work *De solido intra solidum naturaliter contento,* dissertationis prodromus from 1669

---

68 In the appendix of this third edition, the gemstone book of Theophrastos is also printed in Greek and Latin in the context of the gemstone book of Joannes de Laet (Letius) (1581–1649): *Gemmarum et Lapidum Historia: Quam olim editit ANSELMUS BOETIUS de BOOT*, Brugensis, RUDOLPHI II. Imperatoris Medicus, 3rd edition, Lugduni Batavorem, 1617.

69 Ibid., p. 13: '*Lapis itaque est corpus mixtum, inanime, durum, inductile, in aqua non liquabile, & solidum. [...] Lapis itaque alius a natura magnus, alius parvus prodicitur. Parvus alius rarus inventus, alius frequentus: rarus alius durus, alius mollis. Durus alius pulcher, apectuque gratus, alius turpis. Pulcher gemme nomen meretur. Erit itaque gemma lapis parvus, rarus, durus, & pulcher a natura procreatus.*'

laid the foundation for crystallography, which would go on to bloom in the nineteenth century. During his examination of quartz, he discovered the law of the angular constancy of crystals, according to which the surfaces of crystals are always at the same angle to each other, regardless of their size and shape. His work impressively documents the novel approach to scientific knowledge, which drew its conclusions from the precise observation and description of natural objects.[70]

He begins his statements about the crystal with an explanation of the term:

'A crystal consists of two hexagonal pyramids and an intermediate column that is also hexagonal. Here I call terminal solid angles those angles that form the apices of the pyramids but those that are formed by the union of the pyramids with the column I refer to as intermediate solid angles; in the same way, I refer to the planes of the pyramids as terminal planes and the planes of the column as intermediate planes. The plane of the base is a section perpendicular to all the intermediate planes. A plane of the axis is a section in which lies the axis of the crystal, made up of the axes of the pyramids and the axis of the column.' [71]

In the context of this essay, Steno's view of the genesis of crystals is remarkable. Although he mentions the growth of crystals, he clearly distances himself from the concept of a vegetative (plant) growth:

'A crystal grows while new crystalline material is added to the exterior planes of the already formed crystal, so that there is no room at all here for the opinion of those who assert that crystals grow vegetatively, that they draw their nourishment from the side on which they are attached to the matrix, so that the particles thus received from the fluid of the rock and transmitted into the fluid of the crystal are added internally to the crystal particles.' [72]

For him, as the further course of the text shows, the realms of minerals, plants and animals were clearly separated from each

---

70 Nicolaus Steno, '*De Solido ... Prodromus Dissertation on Solids Naturally Contained within a Solid*', in: idem, *Geological Papers*, ed. Gustav Scherz, Odense, 1969, especially pp. 174–81.

71 Ibid., p. 173.

72 Ibid., p. 175. And John G. Winter, *The Prodromus of Nicolaus Steno's Dissertation Concerning a Solid Body Enclosed by Process of Nature within a Solid*, London, 1916, available at: https://archive.org/stream/prodromusnicola00stengoog/prodromusnicola00stengoog_djvu.txt.

other according to the traditional view of a 'Scala naturae'. He understood crystallisation as an immanent process:

'If a solid body is enclosed on all sides by another solid body, of the two bodies that one first became hard which, in the mutual contact, expresses on its own surface the properties of the other surface. Hence it follows:

- *That in the case of those solids, whether of earth, or rock, which enclose on all sides and contain crystals, selenites, marcasites, plants and their parts, bones and the shells of animals, and other bodies of this kind which are possessed of a smooth surface, these same bodies had already become hard at the time when the matter of the earth and rock containing them was still fluid. And not only did the earth and rock not produce the bodies contained in them, but they did not even exist as such when those bodies were produced in them.*
- *That if a crystal is enclosed in part by a crystal, a selenite by a selenite, a marcasite by a marcasite, those contained bodies had already become hard when a part of the containing bodies was still fluid.*
- *That in the earth and rock in which crystalline and petrified shells, veins of marble, of lapis lazuli, silver, mercury, antimony, cinnabar, copper, and other minerals of this kind are contained, the containing bodies had already become hard at the time when the matter of the contained bodies was still fluid; and that, consequently, the marcasites were produced first, then the stones in which the marcasites are enclosed, and finally, the veins of minerals which fill the fissures of the rock.'*[73]

Fossil findings, in particular of shells in the high mountains, did cause excitement in Steno[74] and many of his contemporaries, but they did not shake his confidence in the historical truth of the biblical story of Creation, all the more since he himself was a cleric: *'With regard to the first aspect of the Earth, Scripture and nature agree in this respect, that everything was covered with water; but of how and when it began, and how long it lasted as such, Nature says nothing, while Scripture speaks. That there was aqueous fluid, however, at a time when animals and plants had not yet appeared,*

73 Ibid., pp. 150–1.

74 Ibid., pp. 188–9: *'Among the solids naturally enclosed by a solid, no group occurs more frequently, nor arouses greater doubt than the shells of molluscs.'*

and that the fluid covered everything is proved conclusively by the strata of the higher mountains which are free from all heterogeneous material; the outline of these strata testifies the presence of a fluid; their material bears witness to the absence of heterogeneous bodies; the similarity in materials and outlines of strata from different mountains that are widely separated proves indeed that the fluid was universal.'[75]

It was clear for him that the receding water had left evidence of maritime life in the crevices and hollows of the Earth. Also later flooding, like the biblical flood, proves the veracity of the holy writings:

'When and how the second aspect of the Earth, which was flat and dry, began, Nature is likewise silent, while Scripture speaks; moreover, Nature's assertion that such an aspect of the Earth did exist at one time is confirmed by Scripture when it teaches that waters gushing from one source overspread the whole Earth.'[76] The genesis story of the Bible stood as the authoritative reference work of the Earth's history, more or less explicitly until the second half of the eighteenth century.[77]

Robert Boyle addressed the subject in 1673, after reading the books of de Boodt and Steno, whom he acknowledged thoroughly in his preliminary remarks. He criticised the gemstone medicine of Antiquity and the Middle Ages as scientifically unsupported and trusted instead the analytical investigation and experiments regarding crystallisation. His greatest achievements regarding the goals of this work are presumably that he embraced crystallisation as a theme of interest, inspired by Kepler's 'New Year's

---

75 Ibid, pp. 204–5.

76 Ibid.

77 This is proved not only by the *Neptuniums*, persistently represented by Abraham Gottlob Werner as well as by Goethe until the early nineteenth century, but also, for example, by the declaration attached to the *L'histoire naturelle* [General Natural History] by George-Louis Leclerc de Buffon on 12 March 1751: *'That it never occurred to me to contradict the texts of the Holy Scriptures, that I would confidently believe everything that there is told about creation, thus probably with the intention of the order of the times, as is told about the circumstances of the events themselves, and that I would let go of everything that I may have said in my book contrary to the formation of the earth or to the Mosaic Laws in general, I declare my assumed proposition of the formation of planets to be nothing but a philosophical premise.'* Translated from the German edition: *Herrn von Buffons allgemeine Naturgeschichte: Eine freye mit einigen Zusätzen vermehrte übersetzung nach der neuesten französ. Ausg. von 1769*, Frankfurt/Main, 2008, p. 990.

Greeting' addressing the crystal formation of snow. He was drawn, in an analogue manner, to crystal forms in an interrelationship with metals and especially the alchemistic 'Tria Principa' of sulphur, salt and mercury that he created experimentally in a trial arrangement, which in turn encouraged Newton to recreate similar experiments.[78] Crystallisation thus inevitably became a phenomenon of living nature that cannot be segregated solely from plant or animal life. The focus is rather on the question of the transition between the inorganic realm of nature and the two organic realms and whether it is not a structural feature common to all 'realms of nature'. In this manner the crystal becomes a testimony to the processes of change in the earth that are not degenerative but rather demonstrate growth instead. In his gemstone book, the results showing crystal growth of salts and metals flowed out of other research areas into his research paper. Of the causes for crystallisation, he saw 'petresent liquors' or 'petresent spirits' that, for their part, turned liquid matter into crystals when they came into contact with it. His chemical investigations could be seen as exemplary for the emerging modern natural sciences and deserve an in-depth accounting of. They mirror the 'alchemistic' knowledge of that epoch, whose in-depth accounting exceeds the capacity of the framework of this accounting.[79] Based upon the work that Boyle illuminated, it cannot just be about classification during the scientific investigation of gemstones but about fundamental, structural, legitimate questions of natural science.[80]

---

78 For Newton's experiments with Regulus Antimonis stellatus, see Betty Jo Teeter Dobbs, *The Foundations of Newton's Alchemy*, Cambridge, UK, 1975, pp. 146–56. Dobbs shows that Newton suspected the action of magnetic corpuscles in the crystalline constellations of antimony in search of the mechanical causes of gravitation in these experiments. Robert Boyle had researched the Regulus Martis stellatus; see p. 62 of the English edition of his *Specimen de Gemmarum Origine & Virtutibus: In quo proponuntur & historice illustrantur quaedam conjecturae circa consistentiam materiae Lapidum Praetiosorum & subjecta, in quibus eorum Praecipuae virtutes consistunt*, Hamburg, 1673, reprint: Mannheim, 2018, an essay about the origin and virtues of gems.

79 Boyle 1673 [note 78].

80 This scientific concept is clearly in contradiction to the descriptive scientific 'mainstream', which develops in the period that followed and which is represented in geology by researchers like de Boodt or Werner, and in biology by Linné. See also Michel Foucault, *The Order of Things: An Archaeology of the Human Sciences*, New York, 1970, Chap. 5. However, Foucault seems to me to underestimate the long-term relevance of the 'other side' of modern science.

Boyle's hypothesis concerning 'invisible particles'[81] seems to be, from today's perspective, a somewhat peculiar deliberation. It is, however, an assumption that the epoch in which the literal truth of the Christian cosmogony of Genesis, according to which God created the world out of nothing in six days, is increasingly shaken by the fossil finds of maritime life in the mountains. If the narrative of Genesis was to be understood metaphorically, the initial divine act of creation must already have laid the substantial foundations for the later development of the world. For this reason, intrinsic particles that jump-start the development and continuity of the matter are necessary. In the epoch of the Copernican Revolution, this issue and therewith also the question of the literal veracity of the Bible were increasingly implemented. It was not just a question of power or about the freedom of natural science research, which were pointedly visible in the cases of Giordano Bruno and Galileo Galileo; it was, from ecclesiastical and natural science perspectives, to a large extent about questions of faith, which moved prominent advocates of both camps. René Descartes, in his treatise 'Prima Philosophia',[82] was not the only one to represent the certainty of God's existence as the origin of all knowledge. Isaac Newton (1642–1726) also, throughout his life but especially in his doctrine on gravitation, repeatedly raised the question of how God influenced the course of the world. Betty Jo Teeter Dobbs discovered, through many years of analysis, especially in the later alchemistic works of Newton's, that '*two tentative solutions to the problem of a cause for gravity emerged in Newton's later years. One was that the omnipresent Supreme Deity subsumed gravity directly. The other was that an intermediate agent existed between God and the world, an agent that could account for gravity (as the vegetal spirit, an intermediary between God and the world, accounted for vegetation), but the agent for gravity had to be of such a nature that it would not constitute a drag on the motions of the heavenly bodies. [...] The stoic pneuma had become a Divine*

81 Boyle 1673 (note 78), Engl. ed. p. 55: '*I elsewhere shew, that ev'n in the Figures of Allom, Vitriol and other Salts, that are so curiously and Geometrically shap'd, there is no necessity to fly to a distinct Architectonick principle / – but that those Bodies themselves may receive their shapes from the Coalition of such singly invisible Corpuscles, as by the Motion of the Fluid, wherein they did swim, and by divers assistant Circumstances, are determin'd to stick together rather in that manner than in another.*'

82 René Descartes, 'Meditationes de Prima Philosophia', in idem, *Philosophische Schriften in einem Band*, Hamburg, 1996.

Mind, immediately present to every particle of matter in the universe, guiding operations of matter from moment to moment, and always intelligently aware of everything in the universe.' [83]

What is mostly overlooked is that in the seventeenth century, similar ideas of a divine 'Spirit' particle, which has evolved the divine will in world history since the first act of creation, had long been represented in some circles of the Catholic clergy. The most prominent proponent was the Jesuit Athanasius Kircher (1602–1680), who was appointed in 1663 by Ferdinand II as the imperial court mathematician and successor to Kepler and, after failing in the appointment, moved to Rome and worked in an institutional order for natural sciences, studying, among other things, magnetism. One of his guiding concepts in the natural sciences was the godly panspermia. Thomas Leinkauf researched these guiding concepts in-depth:

'The central factual circumstances for the panspermia idea is that God sets an absolute primordial base of all natural things, as "materia primordialia", or rather, "materia chaotica", which in and of itself (unica) receives its entire primal shape through the godly spirit and is everlasting in this characterisation. [...] The formative, structured, and ordered diversity of forms in the individual formations' driving force of panspermia, which, as shown, is primordial, conditioned through the godly spirit, steps forth for Kircher especially clearly at the critical point of their internal differentiation: in the dichotomy of a virtus plastica and a virtus magnetica. They impart God's originally conceptualised contingent of shapes (species) and laws (classification and organisational forms) with their respective actual statuses in the world, so that in principle this contingent is conserved. The malleable properties are thereby responsible for the individual form and composition (it impacts the parameters forma, figura, colour), the magnetic, in contrast to the relationships of these individual forms amongst themselves (vis attractiva/regulativa).' [84]

---

83 Betty Jo Teeter Dobbs and Margaret C. Jacobs, *Newton and the Culture of Newtonianism*, New York, 1995, pp. 50–1. For a more in-depth insight into the subject, see Betty Jo Teeter Dobbs, *The Janus Faces of Genius: The Role of Alchemy in Newton's Thought*, Cambridge, UK, 1991; Lioba Wagner, *Alchemie und Naturwissenschaft: Über die Entstehung neuer Ideen an der Reibungsfläche zweier Weltbilder: Gezeigt an Paracelsus, Robert Boyle und Isaac Newton*, Würzburg, 2011.

84 Thomas Leinkauf, Mundus Combinatus: Studien zur Struktur der barocken Universalwissenschaft am Beispiel Athanasius Kirchers SJ (1602–1680), Berlin, 2009, pp. 100 ff.

Although Kircher, who was guided by Paracelsian views, thus stood like Boyle or Newton in the 'alchemical' tradition – which is mostly denounced as unscientific – the cleric's ideas covered a wide dissemination.

The French mathematician, natural scientist and encyclopaedist George-Louis Leclerc Comte de Buffon (1707–1788) was received as a pioneer of biology across Europe with his thirty-six volumes of *L'histoire naturelle*.[85] The mathematician, geodesist, astronomer, natural scientist and philosopher Pierre Louis Mooren de Maupertuis (1698–1754) also had a not inconsiderable influence as temporary director of the Prussian Academy of Sciences in Berlin.

In Berlin 1754 Maupertuis wrote his treatise composed under the pseudonym Dr Baumann, entitled *Système de la nature*:

'Do plants, minerals and also metals have similar origins? Does their creation not bring us to the creation of other organised objects? Do we not see, under our very eyes, the something that, in the germination of plants and in the matrix of animals, seems similar; if the most subtle parts of a salt are in an arbitrarily selected liquid that allows them to move and combine, do they actually combine and form homogenous, cubic, pyramidal bodies that are of the same character of the selfsame salt? Crushing these bodies, ground to a powder, breaks the bond between the components; these separated parts, swimming in the same liquid, will shortly return to their original configuration, and the same homogenous bodies will arise again. If, however, the overly simple shape of these bodies prevent you seeing the analogism between the one that can be found again, between the generation of them and that of the plants and animals, combining silver particles, saltpetre and quicksilver, then you will see the emergence of this wonderful plant that chemists call the 'tree of Diana', whose genesis may deviate from that of a common tree, in that it takes place patently. This type of tree appears to be to other trees what animals are to others that develop outside of the customary generations, generations like polyps, possibly tapeworms, roundworms, the elongated mealworms; if it is true, then these animals are a composition of components that were not yet animals of the same species.'[86]

85 Georges-Louis Leclerc de Buffon, *Histoire naturelle, générale et particulière*, Paris, 1749–1788; German edition see note 77.

86 P. L. M. de Maupertuis, *Œuvres Bd. II*, reprint of the Lyon edition 1768, Hildesheim, 1965, pp. 166 ff.

Buffon pursued a similar tack in his deliberations at the departure point of his *Histoire naturelle* and developed a theory of nature applicable in all sectors of the material existence that originate from God-given vital (organic) particles that are equally vitalising and stimulating for all fields (minerals, flora, fauna). His comprehensive work is permeated with this conception. Buffon not only found conclusive evidence for him in all natural kingdoms but also undertook elaborate experiments on animal and human reproduction, which he explains in detail in section 4 of his *Histoire naturelle* [87] and discusses in relation to laboratory experiments on the 'procreation in vitro' of other contemporary scientists. His views should, in the following, only be addressed in reference to the mineral kingdom, even though his theory is the most impressive when animal life is used to substantiate his theory.

'Upon closer examination, this concept will show that plants and animals have an unexpected congruence with minerals – the salts, for example – and that several other minerals are made up of components that are uniform among themselves, as well as the whole that they create. A kernel of sea salt is a cube that is made up of innumerable other cubes, visible to the eye through a magnifying glass. These small cubes, again, are made up of smaller cubes, visible to the eye through an even stronger magnifying glass. Is it not highly likely that the essential constituent parts of the salt cube must be small cubes that we can never see with our eyes, or reach, not even using our imagination. Animals and plants that reproduce in all their parts and bring their equivalent forth introduce organic bodies that are made up of similar organic bodies, whose essential constituents are, in turn, organic bodies and others like it. With our eyes, all we can see is their accumulated, heaped multitude; their essential constituent parts are only inferences and only recognisable through (previously) determined similarities. / This makes us believe that within nature there must be an innumerable number of organic parts, truly present and alive, whose substance is of the same substance as that of organic beings. Similarly there are many inorganic parts that are similar to the known inorganic bodies.' [88]

Within his encyclopaedic work, Buffon presents a five-volume *Histoire naturelle des minéraux* [89] based on his theoretical concept

87 Buffon 2008, German edition (note 77), p. 497.

88 Ibid, pp. 405 ff.

89 Georges-Louis Leclerc de Buffon, *Histoire naturelle des Minéraux, Tome I–V*, Paris, 1783, vol. 5 (*Traite de l'aimant* [The Treatise on the Magnet]) appeared in 1788.

outlined above. He places a formation theory of minerals prior to his writings about minerals. Fundamentally he identifies two forces that are involved in the genesis of minerals.

'The greatest and first means that nature used to create all these wonders is the universal and pervasive universal strength that gives life through each and every atom of the matter, by giving them mutual influential tendencies that induce them to be drawn together and combine; the other great means is thermal, and this second force is the tendency of dividing what the first force brought together.'[90]

In order to evoke real growth ('augmentation de la matière'),[91] heat is required to 'break up' the inorganic matter on the one hand, and some trace elements of organic material on the other, which seep into the rock as constituents dissolved in water and set the growth process in motion.

'In this manner, every decomposition and all remnants of animal or plant substances not only serve as nutrition for development and emergence of organised beings but function as active material as an effective agent for the formation of minerals; they alone, through their alternative targeting, according to the resistance of the inert material, can give shape to the particles of any mineral, and only a very small amount of molecules are necessary to determine the superficial trace of organisation in the mineral, whose inside it could not affect. For this reason, the bodies, which are always raw in substance, cannot grow by feeding, like organised beings whose entire inner bulk is continually active; therefore it is only possible for them to increase their volume by enlarging the surface aggregation of their parts.'[92]

The crystal – between art symbol and science

Around the year 1800 – which not only marked a political turning point with the French Revolution but also heralded the replacement of German Classicism by Romanticism as well as the beginning of the Industrial Revolution and the triumphal march of the capitalist economic order – it was not only the arts but also the exploding natural sciences that experienced a repositioning. With important discoveries, natural sciences, like physics and chemistry, began their triumphal

---

90 Ibid., *Tome I*, p. 6.

91 Ibid., pp. 12 ff.

92 Ibid., pp. 14 ff.

march. Biology, which up to this point had conducted descriptive and systematic research, would only experience its actual big bang around the middle of the century, with Darwin's theory of evolution. Also in geology, which hitherto understood itself as geognosy, a phase of reorientation began. This was marked by the end of the life of the leading German geologist Abraham Gottlob Werner and was also represented by Goethe throughout his life. René-Just Hauey (1743–1822) set, with his development of the symmetry of crystals, an additional milestone in the development of modern crystallography.[93]

With regard to the symbolic content of the gemstones, in particular the crystal, the outcome is a multilayered tableau:

- Gemstones became commercial industrial products based upon the prototype ideal (faceted) cut outlined above. The value of the stones was determined by the rational principles of the market. The price symbolised its value.
- The historic 'symbolic dowry' continued to carry meaning and affect part of the market value.
- From a scientific point of view, there are two completely diverse concepts:
  a. The descriptive and systemised recording that is, among others, promoted by the Neptunist Werner.
  b. Crystals as growth phenomena of nature in the spirit of panspermia. The theoretical approach that I described above was picked up by Schelling or Carus, for example, and continues to be pursued in the modern bio-genetics field.
- During the Goethe era, especially Romanticism, the crystal was discovered as an art symbol.[94] Among the historically accrued meanings, the crystal was favoured as a vital symbol of an enlivened nature.

The Goethe era also became an age of upheaval for the crystal. While crystal as a metaphor of art was usually reproduced according to the traditional geometric image – despite all the vitalism associated with it – in the natural sciences it took a completely different path with the new biology by becoming the structural manifestation of biological life.

---

93 Released in 1784 with his *Essai d'une theorie de la structure des crystaux*, the first of a variety of treatises about crystals.

94 F.W.J. v. Schelling, 'Über das Verhältnis der bildenden Künste zur Natur' (1807), in *Philosophie der Kunst: Schriften zur Philosophie der Kunst*, Leipzig, 1911, pp. 395–6.

The beginnings of modern crystallography were to be introduced by Johann Wolfgang von Goethe and Carl Gustav Carus, two personalities known from nineteenth-century art who were also ambitious natural scientists. Goethe, famous as a poet, played a more prominent but also more controversial role than Carus the physician. Goethe, who pursued various scientific ambitions far beyond his professional activity as mining minister at the Weimar court, fought in vain for recognition as a scientist.[95] Ultimately he was impassioned for the remainder of his long life for what was known as geognosy, today's geology, which, beginning in the middle of the seventeenth century, temporarily became the leading natural science. The focus of geognosy research was the discovery of the historicity of the Earth – beyond the godly history of creation: the Earth as natural history and as the history of the development of animal and ultimately also human life, as an ascending history of the self-perfection of nature. Goethe not only received and cited the early theories of Buffon, Maupertuis and Robinet concerning the evolution of the Earth[96] and its terrestrial life but also

95 Among the ranks of contemporary natural scientists, Goethe's work as a natural scientist is also usually disparaged as completely unscientific – strangely enough even in contexts such as vol. 3 (pp. 672–3) of the Goethe four-volume handbook (Stuttgart and Weimar 1997 special edition) or in a commentary by Carl Friedrich von Weizsäcker on Goethe's *Begriffe aus der Naturwissenschaft* in vol. 13 (pp. 539–55) of the fourteen-volume *Werke: Hamburger Ausgabe*. His concepts of crystal and crystallisation are described in the handbook as almost absurd. Weizsäcker looks after the ingenious poet prince's scientific, amateurish naivety: '*But is the gesture of nature an artistic means of the poetic imagination? Doesn't the poet here understand something out of the movement of his own soul, where in itself nothing at all can be understood? / The man of the rational age must ask this question. Only he should be slow with the answer. The poet hits an old rock here. The source, which he opens up once more, in freedom and how playfully, has soaked mankind in the great bondage of the mythical age. At that time the difference between the inside and the outside had not yet been pronounced. Sign and soul, sign and meaning were still, contrary to what we can imagine, one.*' (Ibid., p. 554)

96 This concept of evolution also has, in some ways, ancient and high medieval predecessors. Aristotelian kinematics knows the possibility of the transmutation of elements, in which one element can migrate into another (neighbouring) element – for instance, solid ice into fluid water and into aeriform steam. Albertus Magnus describes in this manner the formation of crystals from ice (cold moisture) through the development of hot dryness (from the sun at high altitude). On this theoretical basis, medieval alchemists set out on laboratory experiments to generate the 'stone of knowledge', a primeval matter from which all other materials can evolve through the transmutation of the mineral. The affinity with the Faustian laboratory is apparent.

developed his own intense geo-scientific, physical, botanical and medicinal research projects, whose elements he combined into a natural philosophical morphology. Less well known than his colour theory are his laboratory experiments and his microscopic works in 1785 and 1786. Apparently Goethe's primary concern was not the phenomena of crystallisation as forms of transition from inorganic 'life' to plants, or the exemplary dynamic self-expression of nature. Many had believed to have discovered inorganic life forms in the 'growth' of silver crystals on the 'tree of Diana', on the dendrites of *pietra fungata*, a truffle-like growth. Inspired by these works, especially presumably due to the dissertation of the German biologist Wilhelm Friedrich von Gleichen-Russwurm,[97] he dedicated himself to the microscopic examination of primitive life forms concerning the transition from inorganic to organic life. The reasons why Goethe abandoned this research approach in September 1776 with his sudden departure for Italy are unknown to this day.[98] Goethe warned, however, against too hasty analogies, which already recognised mineral crystallisation as a form of vegetation.

'To me, they seem to give too much value to these effects of nature; they wish to raise these crystallisations to the rank of the vegetal. [...] We should, it seems to me, pay more attention to how the things to which we strive to achieve differentiate from one another, instead of how they resemble each other. Differentiating is more difficult, more arduous than finding similarities, and if we have differentiated effectively then the objects thereupon compare themselves. If you begin with finding things similar or the same, in that case, one becomes too attached to the hypothesis or idea and overlooks the criteria whereby things are very different from one another.'[99]

---

97 Wilhelm Friedrich von Gleichen-Russwurm, *Abhandlung über die Saamen- und Infusionsthierchen und über die Erzeugung*, Nuremberg, 1778. French: *Dissertation sur la génération, les animalcules spermatiques et ceux d'infusions avec observations microscopiques sur le sperme et sur differentes infusions*, Paris 1799. Like Buffon he also regards 'seed animals' as germs of human life. In his dissertation he describes, among other things, crystal formations in infusion solutions during the genesis of semen animals (see pp. 9 ff., French edition).

98 See especially the dissertation of Margrit Wyder, *Goethes Naturmodell: Die Scala naturae und ihre Transformationen*, Cologne, Weimar and Vienna, 1998, which discusses the natural philosophy of Goethe that sets the context in the scientific history of the eighteenth and nineteenth centuries. On Goethe's *infusion animalcules* see ibid. pp. 191–4.

99 Goethe, LA 1, section II, p. 27.

In 'geognosy' Goethe did not develop any scientific interest beyond the Werner research approach.[100] The reason he did not concern himself with the crystallisation theme was by no means due to lack of interest. It lay more likely with the methodological procedure of predecessors like Buffon, who approached crystallisation from the vegetal side of the issue.[101]

After the end of his basic research on the transition from inorganic to organic life, Goethe, as a renowned natural scientist, dealt with the morphology of plants and for years embarked on a (futile) search for the primordial plant from which all plants originate. However, he was still a mining specialist and mineralogist. He had

---

100 Werner's permanent accomplishments did not result from the theory of Neptunism but out of a descriptive system of minerals and earthen layers. This research approach was followed with enthusiasm by Goethe as a collector into old age. Crystallisation was for Goethe and Carus not only a metaphor for natural phenomena but also an immediate expression of a dynamically developing nature that, as Leibniz said, makes no jumps. Both can refer to considerable comprehensive natural sciences accomplishments, even though Goethe, especially, with an exorbitant contempt for his scientific accomplishments, tormented himself. The two graduates moved with surety among natural-philosophical ideas, despite Novalis spending two years studying at the Mountain Academy in Freiberg and later working as a saline assessor and member of the saline directorate in Weissenfels/Saale – therefore, like Goethe, he moved in the scientific tradition of Abraham Gottlob Werner (1749–1817), who was teaching there at the time. At least until the turn of the century into 1800, they were abreast of the 'geognostic' science of the time. In the geosciences of this epoch, a dispute raged between Neptunists and Plutonists. The former were based on a development of the earth and the earthly life from the ur-ocean, in which the mainland was deposited in four deposition periods and emerged with receding water and eroded due to weather influences. The latter set volcanism at its beginning. Carus also had contact with Werner. The Romantic Ludwig Tieck, who lived in Dresden, was also a friend of Carus's for many decades, which suggests a scientific exchange. Even though Neptunism was a very popular religion at the beginning of the nineteenth century, it was scientifically refuted at the beginning of the nineteenth century, and the idea of an 'organic' development according to a spiritual idea or a natural law has survived to the present day.

101 Goethe did not pursue his thesis any further, not least because he had no real chance of microscopic research due to the insufficient developments in scientific aids (microscopy): the twentieth-century research potential concerning his crystallisation thesis has principally recognised his work as the predecessor of organic life. See Monod 1972 (note 64). The molecular biologist and Nobel Prize recipient in medicine asks about the transition from inorganic to organic growth in his book: '*There was a "Platonic" ambition in the systematic search for anatomical invariants to which the great nineteenth-century naturalists, Cuvier and Goethe, devoted themselves.*' Ibid., p. 101.

an in-depth preoccupation with granite. Not least he was moved by the grandeur of the Swiss Alps, through which he travelled with his princely friend and employer from Weimar. Even though Goethe had great interest in geognosy and mineralogy for the greater part of his life, he showed very little specific interest in gemstones. He considered this to be a less interesting chapter of geoscience. The following rather vague statement has been handed down: *'It seems to me as if nature, as it can never give up the higher chemical effects in the inorganic realm, has reserved the refinement of form and colour for itself in every epoch of time.'* [102]

Goethe saw, in general, a legitimately created dynamic moment in nature:

'The fulfilment, however, that he is missing is the contemplation of the two great driving forces of nature: the terms polarity and ascension, all polarity of matter, insofar as we regard these materially, then they increase contrast; insofar that we imagine them, they belong. It is in eternal attraction and repulsion, and this is continually striving to ascend. However, because matter is never without spirit, and the spirit can never exist and still be effectual without matter, so the material increases, so the spirit does not allow it to attract or repel, in the same manner as the spirit is capable of thinking alone, has sufficiently united in order to want to separate again.' [103]

In the context mentioned above, he notes in relation to Leonhard on the formation of gemstones:

'All mountainous masses separate and form cosmically; within the mass, however, there is a tendency to represent oneself in one's own way. / We crystallised granite within the granite [...]. We crystallised gneiss within gneiss [...], crystals are formed in the porphyry, similar to the original form. [...] / This striving, with which the mass endeavours to ennoble itself, moves through the epochs to this very day. The newest gypsum (plaster) is equally porphyry as the porphyry itself [...] yes, the metals themselves, tin, tungsten and those related, have taken on form through mass. However, I cannot help but notice that this can appear as either massive or plentiful. / The second one is to be noted: the refinement in freedom, when the mass leaves spaces that the types of gas circulating eternally in the same ones from the earliest to the latest times dissolve,

---

102 Remarks to Leonhard on 28 April 1816. J. W. Goethe, *Werke*, vol. 13, Hamburg and Munich, 2000, *notes on the chapter on geology*, p. 603.

103 J. W. Goethe, remarks on the aphoristic essay 'Natur'; ibid., p. 48.

liberate, transform, make sociable the peculiarities of the mountain. Here these bodies, which we call precious stones, seem to have been created.'[104]

Precisely this process, in which the spiritual principle of ascension into a higher form is realised, was what he called crystallisation – a principle that weaves through Goethe's entire morphology.

It is the question of crystallisation that fascinated him especially. He became, in consideration of fossil findings of organic life in the Alps, a follower of Werner's Neptunist theory concerning the creation of Earth and life from the sea, or rather the primordial soup of the sea. As a supporter of the harmony-influenced conception of nature, his entire life was spent in persistent opposition to volcanic majority opinion. For him, crystallisation becomes a transitional phenomenon between inorganic and organic life. He gave a clear hint in Faust II in the scene in which Faust creates his son as a homunculus in the retort and, enraptured, perceives the phenomenon of crystallisation as the birth process of life.[105]

Goethe's stance was – in his opinion of the creation of the world as a process of organic self-development from inanimate matter all the way to humanity – not outside that of European intellectual history. The Faustian alchemistic act of creation had already been predefined in the Aristotelian concept of the transformability of the elements and was, in Goethe's conception, not just a metaphoric deposit of crystallisation. Crystallisation becomes essentially the book of nature. To read it means to know a part of the code of nature's language that imparts information about the development of nature. Goethe's ideas also surface in many areas of philosophy in German idealism and in the Romantic literature in the first half of the nineteenth century. And above all, in this epoch, the science of crystallography emerges and has characterised our conception of the crystal up to the present time with an almost unmanageable amount of graphic representations.

A somewhat younger contemporary and admirer of Goethe's, a painter and sketch artist but also a physician researching natural

104 J. W. Goethe, concerning the formation of gemstones, ibid., pp. 179–80

105 J. W. Goethe, *Faust*, 2nd act, Laboratory, Verses 6857, 6860 and 6907–6910, Wagner to Mephistopheles:
'When the mysteries of nature are extolled,
We dare reasonably attempt,
And what else could be organised,
We will allow to crystallise.'

science who gained fame as a natural philosopher, continued to pursue Goethe's ideas about morphology: Carl Gustav Carus. Carus, for his part, influenced Goethe with his ideas on morphology, possibly providing him with the keyword for his homunculus scene through the enclosure of a manuscript in his letter to Goethe of 23 November 1823. In the then unprinted introduction of his *Grundzüge allgemeiner Naturbetrachtung* [Main Features of General Nature Observation], he writes:

'But then if the liquid element is of organic creation, then it follows from this that it was alive in the first place, where the solidified material is regarded as a product or a residue of this life in which the animate effect has foundered, as a product which must be dissolved into the original liquid if it is to be newly reanimated and be reconfigurable. / This is the manner in which it happens if in the liquid the tendency towards crystallisation (that is: a polar configuration tendency – life force) becomes active; we must then name the crystallisation itself that arises out of inner principles derived from the substance's movement life, but this life expires in the finally solidified structure of the crystal; it is the residuum, the caput mortuu of life, and as such it cannot in and of itself be more alive; we must see it as dead, and we will in the long or short term see it decay, dissolve, devolve into liquid and thereby it will become able to create new formations as an element. It appeared in this manner and also the layers of our earthly bodies as residues of the original formation of life on this planet; they are thereby dead, and not until their gradual weathering and dissolution are they able to serve as individually organised elemental structures.'[106]

Carus – who had a thoroughly critical, perhaps even ambivalent relationship with Goethe[107] – introduced crystallisation at the preliminary stage of organic life in 1861, almost at the end of his life, in his book *Natur und Idee oder das Werdende und sein Gesetz* [Nature and Idea or the Emergent and its Law]. In this work he refers on the one hand to his contemporary Schelling,[108] but he

106 Stefan Grosche, *Zarten Seelen ist gar viel gegönnt: Naturwissenschaft und Kunst im Briefwechsel zwischen C.G. Carus und Goethe*, Göttingen, 2001, p. 118.

107 Carus was searching apparently, without the desired outcome, to be recognised by Goethe, especially as an artist; Goethe was, however, successful in his pursuit of recognition as a natural scientist by Carus.

108 Carl Gustav Carus, *Natur und Idee oder das Werdende und sein Gesetz*, Vienna, 1861, pp. 55–6: *'All movement and activity, all movements of life, including nature, are only unconscious thinking, or happen in the form of thinking; however, the*

himself instead took the Platonic elemental theory of Timaios as the starting point of his deliberations.

'In contrast to the liquid, the rigid, if it takes shape from its own inner striving, as it were as a contracted and thus condensed mass of an originally spherical entity, always strives first for the five primordial forms of crystal, tetrahedron, hexahedron, octahedron, and dodecahedron or icosahedron, from which (which of course never occur in nature in absolute mathematical purity) all other forms of crystals can develop through partial modification. Universally, on the other hand, just as the solid results from the liquid mechanically subduing itself and crystalline or un-crystalline solidifies as a cause of the liquid solidifying, it becomes necessary to also strive towards the spherical, in the way the nominal hollow spherical shell of the planet itself must have once made itself.' [109]

Eventually he sees in crystallisation the first self-induced form of the organisation of matter and thus life:

'That which crystallises in a definitive characteristic manner is to be rightfully understood as veritably individual. Natural philosophy can thus express the sentence: The first thing, through which the single-cell entity of the later epitellurian creatures is foretold and prepared, is the crystal. / The primary difference, which incidentally forever strictly separates the telluric crystal from all true epitellurian organisms, is that the vitality of these takes place purely in its formation, while in contrast the actual task of the epitellurian organisms' vitality always begins after the conclusion of its formation and is contingent upon a continually ongoing renewal.'

With this concept Carus, and before him also Goethe, were by no means forerunners of anthroposophy or of contemporary esotericism. They were in good academic company. I am the owner of *Naturgeschichte des Mineralreichs* [Natural History of the Mineral

---

more legitimately it shows itself in nature, the more spiritual it essentially appears to be. The optical phenomena, for example, are already a geometry whose lines are of light, and a perfect theory of nature (natural philosophy) would be that whose force determines the direction of life in all of nature (for example, in an idea of godly origin; however, we are reminded at the same time of something very much older, pointed out by Plato, in which the following is stated concerning the genesis of movement: 'that which is continually in motion is immortal; that which moves other or is moved by other, and therefore has a movement phase, also has a phase of life. Only that which moves itself, because it never leaves itself, will never stop being moved, but also all else that is moved is the spring and source of movement. The beginning is, however, unrisen'. See Plato, Phaedrus, Chap. 245 St.3.C.

109 Ibid., pp. 45–6.

Kingdom] from 1842, authored by Professor Dr Nepomuk Fuchs, former holder of the chair for mineralogy at the Royal University Munich. He writes concerning the genesis of crystals:

'The process in which crystals are formed is called crystallisation; the crystals are often also called crystallisations. The unknown cause of this odd and wonderful formation is designated with the term "force of crystallisation". All efforts to elucidate it further have thus far been, and more than likely will always remain, fruitless. The force of crystallisation is, we would like to state, in the kingdom of inorganic objects that which is in the organic kingdom life force. / The crystallisation formation requires an amorphous precondition, since it is reasonable that, prior to the formation of a regular body, it is out of the question if you do not assume that it was previously formed irregularly. The most advantageous is the same, the phase in the form of a drop, when the object/body is molten, or in water or also dissolved in another liquid. Many bodies can also migrate out of a steam-like condition to the crystalline.'[110]

After listing several examples, Fuchs made a footnote which is representative of the development of crystallography at that time:

'In recent times, crystals have become the subject of many different observations, and mathematics has found a wide field of application. Crystallography has thus been elevated to a special scientific doctrine, which different crystallographers have elaborated in different ways, almost each forming its own terminology. They all extract from this doctrine only as much as is needed for their mineralogical purposes in order to make an identifying determination and name it mineralogical crystallography. The founder of mathematical crystallography is Hauy; in recent times it has been further developed by Weiß, Mohs, Naumann and others, and the diversity of crystallisations has been traced back to six systems. Earlier Werner and Romé de l'Isle had rendered outstanding services to mineralogical crystallography.'[111]

Mineralogical textbooks for the practice of the gemstone trade testify to the complete penetration of descriptive, mathematical crystallography in Germany as far back as the 1860s,[112] which does not contribute to the clarification of the causes of crystal formation

---

110 Joh. Nep. Fuchs, *Naturgeschichte des Mineralreichs*, Kempten, 1842, p. 13.

111 Ibid., p. 15, footnotes. Werner is the leading protagonist of Neptunism, to whom Goethe ultimately refers throughout his life.

112 See Karl Emil Kluge, *Handbuch der Edelsteinkunde für Mineralogen, Steinschneider und Juweliere*, Leipzig, 1860.

but only places crystallography in the representation of the phenomenon on a mathematical basis. The different crystals can now – this is symbol politics as well – be named on a 'mathematical basis'.

In the second half of the nineteenth century, morphology in the tradition of Goethe and the idea of an evolution of nature, in which crystallisation as a connecting structural principle between inorganic and organic life, also from a scientific point of view, was repeatedly brought into the discussion. At this point I would like to mention Ernst Haeckel (1834–1919) on the one hand and Otto Lehmann (1855–1922) on the other. The physician, zoologist, philosopher and freethinking Haeckel published his main work *Generelle Morphologie* [General Morphology] in 1866 and his work *Kristallseelen* [Crystal Souls],[113] which he simply dedicated to the life principle, the crystalline, in 1917. He placed three citations from Goethe ahead of his work, with which he established the specific reference upon his morphology. He regards the crystal as a *'morphological individuality [that is] limited in time and space. [...] Every crystal form, as individual or singular (no matter if equally chemically homogenous or mixed), originates in a "germ", i.e. a central molecular group, and grows to a certain size. This individual maximum size is different for the individual species; it does not, however, exceed its upward limitations. There are, for this reason, numerous crystals (namely biological crystals) which remain microscopically small and do not even reach one millimetre in diameter. Some ancient mono-crystals (for example of rock crystal) reach a diameter of several metres and a weight exceeding a hundredweight.'* [114]

The physicist Otto Lehmann[115] discovered liquid crystals in 1904, thereby providing the scientific basis for LCDs. *'The analogies that show themselves between the formative and driving forces of liquid crystals and life forms cause me to designate the myelin crystals of the paraazoxycinnamic acid ethyl ester as what appear to be living crystals; the well-known and famed biologist E. Haeckel defined them as actual life, and perhaps one day physiology will be able to prove that those analogies are actually related to or are based on the identity of the effective molecular forces. Of great interest is, apparently, that the so-called bio-crystals that occur in living substances orient themselves according to the laws of the organism, as if the*

113 Ernst Haeckel, *Kristallseelen*, Leipzig, 1917.

114 Ibid., pp. 4–5.

115 Otto Lehmann, *Flüssige Kristalle und ihr scheinbares Leben*, Leipzig, 1921, pp. 56–7.

molecules of the living substance were also receiving a directional force that directs the molecules of firmer crystals upon the formation of the crystal germs and thus must be related to the directional force of the crystal molecules. One must also note that liquid crystalline substances, like oleates, cholesterol connections, lecithin, phrenosin, choline etc., are part of the living substance or are found within it, as well as swellable crystals of protein, haemoglobin etc., and that colloids like fibrin, gelatine, cellulose, horn, chitin etc., made up of very small crystals, similar to the liquid crystals, soft small crystalline fibrils or micelles, are only set apart from uniform crystals by the heterogeneous (colloidal) mixture with other substances.'

At the same time, at the beginning of the century, he gave new life again to the discussion concerning the life principle of 'crystallisation'. Also in this epoch the art symbol of the crystalline was fertilised quite directly and enduringly from natural science. And from a natural sciences perspective, it was definitely not meant to be metaphorical. The change of crystallisation from physics to the biosciences was becoming apparent, not only with Carus and Haeckel – both were also doctors of medicine. And during Lehmann's and Haeckel's time, the natural sciences even caught up with Carus's view that the crystal was the conserved status of a past life process.

The philosopher Hans Blumenberg points out that Friedrich Miescher (1844–1896), the discoverer of nucleic acid (1869), shared this opinion: 'Miescher also orients himself on the familiar: he tends to understand the structure-forming process from the analogy of crystallisation and the role of the "core". Everything that was everyday life, as an heir or also the father, is recognised through the progeny and under no circumstances can rest upon the mere induction of coagulation and crystallisation. The "nucleus" appears to have been underestimated in this "role".'[116] Further current research has meanwhile, among other things, confirmed the crystalline structure of DNA and of insulin – that of organic substance.[117] This is about not just a fringe phenomenon but a central theme of molecular biology. It is about the basic crystalline structures at the doorstep of organic life, which Jacques Monod, one of the first-class contemporary molecular biologists and a Nobel Prize winner, stated in generally understandable terms:

---

116 Hans Blumenberg, *Die Lesbarkeit der Welt*, Frankfurt/Main, 1986, p. 387.

117 See https://de.wikipedia.org/wiki/kategorie:kristallographie and www.chemie.de, Chemie-Lexikon, keyword 'Kristallographie'.

'The DNA's overall structure is the simplest and likeliest to be adopted by a macromolecule formed by linear polymerization of similar radicals: It is a helix strand defined by two symmetry processes – a shift and a twist. The DNA molecule can therefore be regarded as a fibrillar crystal because of the regularity of its overall structure. But if one considers its finer structure, it ought rather to be called an aperiodic crystal, since the sequence of the base pairs is non-repetitive. It is important to stress that the order is completely 'free' in the sense that it is not restricted by the overall structure, which can contain all possible sequences. / As we have just seen, the forming of this structure compares very closely with that of a crystal. Each sequential element in one of the two strands acts the part of a crystalline seed which chooses and orients the molecules that spontaneously link themselves to it, ensuring the crystal's growth. If artificially separated, two complementary strands will spontaneously reform the specific complex, each of them almost unerringly choosing its partner from among thousands or millions of other sequences.' [118]

It concerns the theme of the fluent transition between the inanimate and animate realms of nature that Goethe researched in weeks of laboratory experiments in the mid 1780s in his search for the primordial plant and the transition from plant to animal – and which inevitably failed because of the lack of suitable technical testing equipment.

This turning point in the history of the crystalline provides a considerable amount of art historical research, a rich opportunity for confirmation – especially the natural sciences evolution theories at the turn of the century and increasingly the public opinion which flowed into, for example, the field of social Darwinism.

In the twentieth century the interest in crystallisation hardly decreased within the natural sciences. Undaunted it still seemed to be about the search for the language of nature. Two aspects are remarkable: the transition of the crystal in the biosphere and the form of the scientific 'objective' representation. This is accompanied by the change of examination instruments – from the human eye to the electron microscope – and thus the change of perspective from spatial, geometric representation to the sphere of digital analogy, namely the dual number code of 1 and 0.

From my elaborations it will hopefully become clear that the art symbol of the crystal in Romanticism and in modern art

118 Monod 1972 (note 64), pp. 101–2.

after 1900 was fed directly from natural science and has reached its present metaphorical meaning possibly only in the course of art historical interpretation to a growing extent. As delightful as Johannes Grave's reference to the scientific context of Goethe's works – and in particular to Carus's views – is,[119] the curious thing on the other hand is the still widespread misinterpretation of Goethe's very modern position, critical of scientific positivism.[120]

From the findings up to now, it is apparent that the development of the crystal to an art symbol of modern times had a considerable development time in natural philosophy and finally in the modern natural sciences, albeit, however, with the relativisation of contemporary gemology, as long as it has developed into an interest-led auxiliary science of gemstone economics. On the road from Expressionism to abstraction, around the turn of the nineteenth century, particularly, it became a symbol of awakening and vitality. This turn to a vitalist interpretation of crystallisation is – caused foremost through the works of Regine Prange – frequently reworked in art history discourse. Since this information is readily available, there is no need to elaborate on it. I would, however, like to address the 'dark side of the crystal', or rather the 'black crystal', again.

Crystalline thinking

Whereas in the second part of this contribution, the unethical interaction of rationalism and economy was discussed in relation to 'crystalline thinking', some contemporary reference to this 'unholy' symbiotic connection of aesthetics, science and economy will now be pointed out. The research results of Monod and of molecular biology led to remarkably pessimistic conclusions by Baudrillard for the future of humanity. He saw in the convergence of the genetic-cybernetic model with the cybernetic structure of electronic media the danger of a manipulated, 'optimised' future of mankind.

---

119 Johannes Grave, 'Zur Faszinationsgeschichte des Kristallinen in der Romantik: Naturforschung und Landschaftsbild bei Carl Gustav Carus', in *Stein aus Licht: Kristallvisionen in der Kunst*, exhib. cat. Art Museum Bern, ed. Mathias Frehner and Daniel Spanke, Bern, 2015, pp. 22–31.

120 The basis for this erroneous assessment apparently lies in a deep prejudice that the natural scientific methods of empiricism and rationality are foreign to the arts. Therefore artists cannot be good scientists. However, it seems to be a mutual prejudice: Goethe, for his part, refused to acknowledge the physician Carus as an artist.

His fears weren't as far-fetched or even as paranoid as the career of the German misnomer of 2010 *Alternativlos* [lack of alternatives][121] indicates, which meanwhile belongs to the preferred political 'decision-making aids'. The transfer of the natural law of inevitability in the sphere of human endeavour had, in fact, triggered a long list of crimes against humanity in the history of the twentieth century. The marine biologist Haeckel, whom we have just met as an enthusiast of biocrystals and as an artist, was – along with many others – a representative of eugenics and became a precursor of German social Darwinism, with the semantic sense of 'opposition is counted as absurd and meaningless'. Even Carus was a proponent of a white superior race. Goethe mentioned that nature was working upon its own perfection. This paradigm of natural-law evolution towards perfection, its transfer to the sphere of social relationships under the elimination of the ethic components of human actions, such as freedom of choice and responsibilities, apparently prompted later generations to assist nature in its perfection in a criminal fashion. Without diminishing the unsurpassed criminal acts of the Nazis against the European Jews, Sinti and Roma, and people with disabilities, would you be surprised if I now began with a recounting of what 'civilised' countries are doing with eugenics programmes – for example, with the forced, mass sterilisation of women in the name of 'demographic development'? Since the days of Plato, it has been a common truism that truth, good and the beautiful are insolubly connected. Goethe often proclaimed this reciprocal relatedness between science, life practice and art.

Jean Baudrillard, in his theory of the simulacrum [illustration, image][122] fundamentally engaged with the question of convergence of natural science, economics and aesthetics. He suggested that, in essence, every form of a picture of nature – including a theoretical one – is ultimately, under theoretical premises, a designed picture of an objectively existing natural object. In reference to the object, any reproduction, to some extent, results in a loss of substance of the natural object. A picture is a picture, and a natural object

121 https://en.wikipedia.org/wiki/Un-word_of_the_year. The misnomer, or non-word, of the year (German: Unwort des Jahres) is the annual publication of a German word or word group that is considered to be the year's most offensive new or recently popularised term.

122 Baudrillard 1993 (note 50).

will remain a natural object.[123] If a picture is made into a reference object, if, for example, reproductions of the picture are made, then the distance to the real object grows. When applied to faceting a shaped gemstone, it means that, through the transformation of the mineral into a facet-cut gemstone, it consummates a loss of the mineral's substance: the mineral is now a man-made artefact. With each additional formal development carried out for technological reasons – because the stone must have a perfect sparkle – and, above all, through serial and mechanical reproduction, the mineral goes on its way towards becoming 'bling'. At the same time it changes into an object of trade, which because of its eventuated loss of substance needs a scientific or even economic certification: this is a stone. However, in the reality of the gemstone trade, certification is about more than that. Since the certification of the authenticity of the material and the physical properties became the basis for the valuation, the last phase of the transformation of the gemstone into a tradable commodity begins here. Therefore its exchange value, even if the exchange of goods is dominated by supply and demand, must be supported by the certificate and its objective facts in order to achieve the highest possible attraction. Since the optical qualities of synthetic gemstones are the same as the natural crystals, then brilliant-cut synthetics can be used in jewellery production without sacrificing optical characteristics, such as brilliance. In this respect, it is only logical in terms of business policy that the former diamond monopolist De Beers is currently starting to trade in synthetic diamonds:

'De Beers admits defeat over man-made diamonds: The world's largest diamond miner is doing the unthinkable: Selling stones produced in a laboratory. De Beers launched a new jewellery brand on Tuesday that features synthetic diamonds, a major reversal for a company that had implored consumers to stick with "real" stones.' [124] and *'De Beers, which almost single-handedly created the allure of diamonds as rare, expensive and the symbol of eternal love, now wants to sell you some party jewellery that is anything but. /*

---

123 Unfortunately it was also stone cutting, which until the Rococo period could rightly be counted among the plastic arts, that in the nineteenth century liberated itself from the fetters of taste by means of courtly art and changed to the flourishing bourgeois camp with painting. After the French Revolution, the ruling aristocracy was inexorably heading for its end.

124 And https://bloomberg.com/news/articles/2018-05-29/de-beers-is-said-to-make-u-turn-by-selling-man-made-diamonds.

The company announced today that it will start selling man-made diamond jewellery at a fraction of the price of mined gems, marking a historic shift for the world's biggest diamond miner, which vowed for years that it wouldn't sell stones created in laboratories.' [125]

By taking this step, the company is taking into account of a development to which it has made a significant contribution itself: the transformation of the stone into its certified monetary value necessitates a market split in view of the increasing exploitation of natural gemstone deposits. On the one hand there is a market for natural gemstones traded as investments and, on the other, a market for synthetic gemstones serving the general public. Baudrillard did not, however, insist on this objective determination: *'The great man-made simulacra pass from a universe of natural laws into a universe of forces and tensions, and today pass into a universe of structures and binary oppositions. After the metaphysics of being and appearance, after energy and determinacy, the metaphysics of indeterminacy and the code. Cybernetic control, generation through models, differential modulation, feedback, question/answer, etc.: this is the new operational configuration (industrial simulacra being mere operations). Digitality is its metaphysical principle (Leibniz's God), and DNA is its prophet. In fact, it is in the genetic code that the 'genesis of simulacra' today finds its completed form. At the limits of an ever more forceful extermination of references and finalities, of a loss of semblances and designators, we find the digital, programmatic sign, which has a purely tactical value, at the intersection of other signals ('bits' of information/tests) and which has the structure of a micro-molecular code of command and control.'*[126]

In conjunction with fashion, Baudrillard stated at the same point that the interchangeability of the symbols is a significant premise. *'Contemporary with political economy and like the market, fashion is a universal form. In fashion, all signs are exchanged just as, on the market, all products come into play as equivalents. It is the only universalisable sign system, which therefore takes possession of all the others, just as the market eliminates all other modes of exchange. So if in the sphere of fashion no general equivalent can be located, it is because from the outset fashion is situated in an even more formal abstraction than political economy, at a stage*

---

125 See http://money.cnn.com/2018/05/29/news/companies/de-beers-man-made-diamonds/index.html:

126 Baudrillard 1993 (note 50) p. 78.

when there is not even any need for a perceptible general equivalent (gold or money) because there remains only the form of general equivalence, and that is fashion itself. Or even a general equivalent is necessary for the quantitative exchange of value, whereas models are required for the exchange of differences. Models are this kind of general equivalent diffracted throughout the matrices which govern the differentiated fields of fashion. They are shifters, effectors, dispatchers, the media of fashion, and through them fashion is indefinitely reproduced. There is fashion from the moment that a form is no longer produced according to its own determinations, but from the model itself – that is to say, that it is never produced, but always and immediately reproduced. The model itself has become the only system of reference. / Fashion is not a drifting of signs – it is their flotation, in the sense in which monetary signs are floated today.'[127]

In the course of transforming the faceted diamond into the ideal prototype of a decorative object, the decontextualisation of traditional references empties the meaning from it and thus transforms it into a freely floating sign (Baudrillard) that can be exchanged like a monetary sign. At this point, the question raised by Baudrillard cannot be explored in greater depth here.[128] However, at least some of the ethical implications in relation to jewellery and fashion should be mentioned.

Baudrillard's approach shows that the gemstone, with its faceted interpretation as a glittering object (that's how one would describe the operative programme for the brilliant cut) and the prototyping demonstrated, enters into the world of 'as if' things and trompe l'oeils, the simulation of reality, at the latest during the Baroque period – thus nearly exactly into the time frame in which this ornamental form emerged: the Baroque. Fifty years previously, Walter Benjamin[129] established that the technically produced and reproduced image causes the observer to verify the reality and the reality by means of the image.

This is also not the time to discuss the ornament. Nevertheless I would not like to omit two passages from Siegfried Kracauer's famous essay 'The Mass Ornament', which he wrote in 1927 around

---

127 Ibid., pp. 112–3

128 See Baudrillard 1993 (note 50), pp. 81–2; Monod 1972 (note 64), p. 100.

129 Walter Benjamin, *The Work of Art in the Age of Mechanical Reproduction*, Frankfurt/Main, 1935.

the time of the Tiller Girls films, one of the most successful dance groups of American revues of the 1920s with a worldwide iconic role model function. He wrote: *'From the perspective of reason, the same process of abstraction appears to be determined by nature; it gets lost in an empty formalism under whose guise the natural is accorded free reign because it does not let through the insights of reason which could strike at the natural. The prevailing abstractness reveals that the process of demythologization has not come to an end. / Present-day thinking is confronted with the question as to whether it should open itself up to reason or to push on against it without opening up at all.'*[130]

He thus alludes directly to the mythicising of the market, which proceeds according to apparently objectively measurable and abstract laws. The form of expression is the mass-production ornament.

'In the mass ornament nature is deprived of its substance, and it is just this that points to a condition in which the only elements of nature capable of surviving are those that do not resist illumination through reason. [...] The organic center has been removed and the remaining unconnected parts are composed according to laws that are not those of nature but laws given by a knowledge of truth, which, as always, is a function of its time. Similarly, it is only remnants of the complex of man that enter into the mass ornament. They are selected and combined in the aesthetic medium according to a principle which represents form-bursting reason in a purer way than those other principles that preserve man as an organic unity. / Viewed from the perspective of reason, the mass ornament reveals itself as a mythological cult that is masquerading in the garb of abstraction. Compared to the concrete immediacy of other corporeal presentations, the ornament's conformity to reason is thus an illusion. In reality the ornament is the crass manifestation of inferior nature. The latter can flourish all the more freely, the more decisively capitalist Ratio is cut off from reason and bypasses man as it vanishes into the void of the abstract. In spite of the rationality of the mass pattern, such patterns simultaneously give rise to the natural in its impenetrability Certainly man as an organic being has disappeared from these ornaments, but that does not suffice to bring man's basis to the fore; on the contrary, the remaining little

---

130 Siegfried Kracauer, 'The Mass Ornament', in *The Mass Ornament*, trans., ed. and intro Thomas Y. Levin, Cambridge, MA, 1995, p. 82.

mass particle cuts itself off from this basis just as any general formal concept does.'[131]

To a certain extent, those Tiller Girls freed from all physicality as symbols of a desexualised sexuality have been made into lifeless jewels of the art of dancing. Kracauer takes a hard look, mind you, at the style of the popular dance group and at the occasion of his fundamental philosophical commentary concerning the ratio duality in the ornament. One could understand it, in today's context, as indications of crystalline thinking. He oppressively takes aestheticising as a substantial component of fascist self-presentation, even before Walter Benjamin had recognised it and Leni Riefenstahl transcribed it photographically in movies like *Triumph of the Will* (Nuremberg Rally of the NSDAP, 1934). However, Riefenstahl does not first translate the Nazi formations marching in front of Hitler as an ornament: in the enactment of the parade, the troops become ornamental and are the Führer's jewellery – a revealing act of inhuman cynicism, even if, presumably, the parties themselves were experienced as an uplifting act of the Führer cult.[132]

From an aesthetic point of view, a completely different conclusion can be drawn for the natural crystal: the process of the rediscovery of crystal as a material of art can begin with recourse to the above-mentioned path of the crystalline as a paradigm of vital – but not vegetative – growth and its transformation as an art symbol since Romanticism. The renunciation of any dogmatic execution of so-called characteristics of aesthetic quality such as 'clarity' or 'cut' are, however, the prerequisite if one wants to discover the 'artificial' properties of the material.

---

131 Ibid., pp. 82–3.

132 In this context, it would be remiss to fail to mention the term *Reichskristallnacht* [Reich crystal night], a pogrom (devastation, destruction, violent etc.) organised and celebrated by the Nazis against the Jewish population in Germany from 7 to 10 November 1938, which, wiath the plundering of Jewish wealth, initiated the epoch of simultaneous displacement and murder of European Jews with this heinous act.

Regine Prange

Dialectics of the Gloss

Jeff Koons' *Celebration* Series and the Heritage of Andy Warhol

Introduction

In according to the lexical definition, the capacity of a surface to reflect light finds its manifestation. The experience of light can be triggered by smoothly polished or varnished materials of various sorts, such as porcelain, precious metals, plastics, wood or leather, but also by liquids. We find an excess of glamour in the erotic image of the female movie star, as for instance Marlene Dietrich fig. 1. The moist gleam in her eyes refers to the biological origin of the gloss as a sign of vitality and desire, and it competes with the diamonds on her wrist and ear, not to forget her lip gloss and nail polish.

Perhaps it is by accident that Jeff Koons's *Balloon Flower* fig. 2, which belongs to the still unfinished series *Celebration*,[1] has been placed on Marlene-Dietrich-Platz in Berlin. In any case it is a meaningful constellation addressing the main issue his art deals with: the aesthetics of capitalism.[2] We will approach the discussion about the *Celebration* series slowly because we first have to look back on the phenomenon of the gloss in art history and Jeff Koons's appropriation of this theme in his early works. As we will see, Jeff Koons is an artist who is highly aware of history.

1 Jeff Koons has worked on the series *Celebration* since 1994. It is supposed to consist of twenty large sculptures and sixteen paintings.

2 This term is used by Gernot Böhme, *Ästhetischer Kapitalismus*, Frankfurt am Main, 2016. See also, from a materialistic point of view, Markus Metz and Georg Seeßlen, *Kapitalismus als Spektakel oder Blödmaschinen und Econotainment*, Frankfurt am Main, 2012.

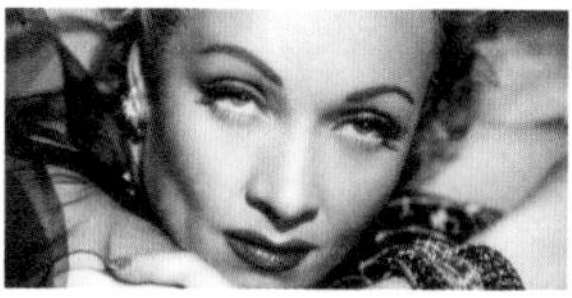

fig. 1

Marlene Dietrich

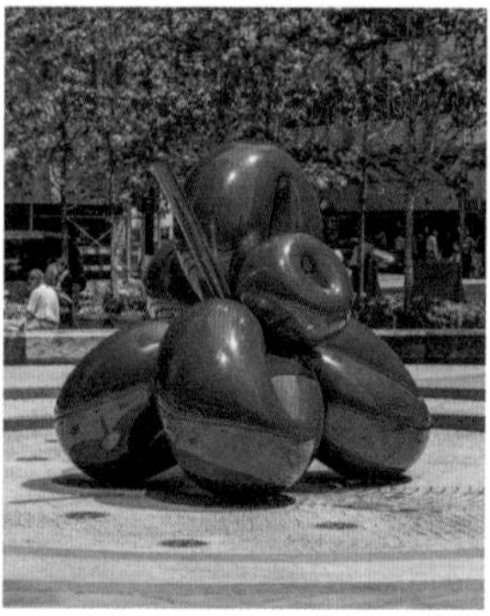

fig. 2

Jeff Koons,
Balloon Flower, (Celebration),
1995–2000

Mirror-polished stainless steel with transparent colour coating, 340 x 285 x 260 cm, 5 unique versions (Blue, Magenta, Yellow, Orange, Red). New York, photo: Reinhold Möller

The Christian occident has subordinated the sensual dimension of shine and glossiness to the functions of feudal power and its religious legitimation, celebrating the glow of light as pure idealisation, as the actual presence of the divine. By means of the overwhelming sensual-mysterious stimulus, the gold surface of Byzantine churches and icons allows the congregation to, so to speak, anticipatively enter kingdom come, which is to be actually reached one day by a pious life. Through the Gothic dematerialisation of the church walls into gemstone-like glimmering glass windows, the promise of the otherworldly love – communion in God – gains a visionary force. A partially secular succession can be seen in the golden shimmer of the Baroque castle as the last historical total work of art. Here the absolute sovereign is the highest authority, the splendour of which Louis XIV, alias the Sun King, does not by accident borrow from the brightest of stars – the radiance of the sun which binds all individuals. The single person does not own itself but belongs to the king, therefore participating in his brilliance and magic.

It is also the humanist art, in contrast to the Byzantine tradition, which renews and updates the rhetoric of the gloss, by means of the technique of oil painting and the autonomous bronze or marble sculpture, which is no longer included as a part of the sacral architecture. It is within this process that a leap in quality from the sacral light to the aesthetic semblance [Schein] happens, which can be best observed within painting. The shine of a numinous otherworldly authority which negates the individual is now replaced by the creative subject, which produces a second nature by their own means of mimesis. While painting in the Middle Ages considered light an inherent quality of colour, immediately emanating a divine force, modern painting works with a secondary nature of light, not used in an unmediated, natural state but rather mediated by the fictional depiction crafted by the artist. Gloss is no longer created by the reflecting surface of gold, nor by transparency or the radiance of the colour itself. Certain surface textures of the depicted pictorial world, of which the artist sometimes imitates the light-absorbing or -reflecting character, now appear glossy. Alberti downright interdicts the – in his days – common use of gold within the pictorial space since it interfered with the trompe l'œil impression. In other words: the primarily sacral image used the preciousness of the light-reflecting material – gold, silver and gems – as an expression of divine creation. Here material and spiritual wealth coincided with

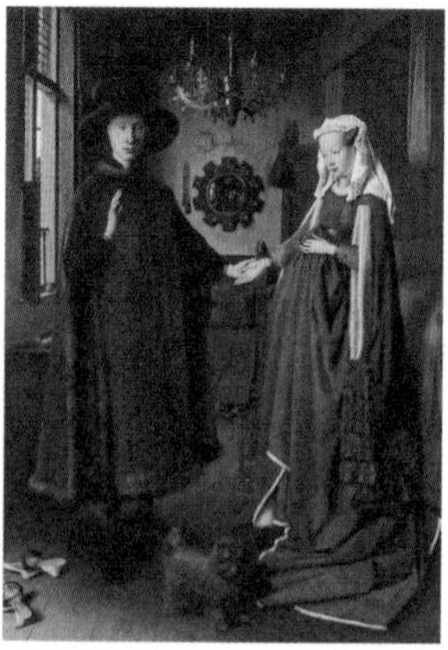

fig. 3

Jan van Eyck,
Arnolfini Wedding Portrait, 1434
Oil on oak, 82 x 60 cm, National Gallery, London

each other. The ars nova of the fifteenth and sixteenth centuries, however, enthrones the artistic as a creative and therefore potentially divine technique. It is no longer merely the gloss of gold as such, which now guarantees the truth and power of a picture. Rather its painterly simulation, as well as the simulation of all other figural surfaces and the atmospheric, light reflecting spaces in between, represents truth. The presence of the divine, staged by means of the golden gloss, is now reinterpreted to be the presence of a here and now of mundane reality, which laid the ground for the emergence of secular genres such as the portrait.

Friedrich Tomberg was probably right when he diagnosed this reference to the mundane within Renaissance painting as the first statement of a bourgeois self-confidence.[3] As a class confidence it no longer defines itself through a divine creature but rather through human nature itself, even if sacral meanings, for instance in the bedroom interior of the Arnolfini Wedding by Jan van Eyck [fig. 3], are still very important. In this picture, which celebrates the moment of the wedding as a bourgeois institution in a ceremonial yet private intimacy, the painting's new claim of presence can be studied exemplarily. With a Latin inscription the artist proves his presence, meaning that he witnessed the marriage. The convex mirror below the inscription shows the two witnesses who validated the marriage settlement, just as if they were facing us. Moreover the mirror is a representation of the painting itself. On the one hand it is in particular the convex, distorting mirror which reminds us that the painting functions in the same way; the mirror objectifies the new ideal of imitation, so to speak. On the other hand it gives occasion to the painterly overtrumping of the mechanic mirror image, which can be immortalised in the painting without distortion, completed by the depiction of the whole room. Gloss now adds up on the objects: the precious mirror, the chandelier, the sumptuous textiles of the decoration and the clothes of the bride and groom. Above all take note of the little dog, positioned right between the two of them. Here already we approach the world of Jeff Koons! The cute pet with the fine shimmering fur completes the bourgeois reality – as a reality based on the production of goods – by expressing its underlying economic principle of the dominance over nature in the sense of its humanisation.

---

3 Friedrich Tomberg, 'Über den gesellschaftlichen Gehalt ästhetischer Kategorien', in *Politische Ästhetik*, Darmstadt/Neuwied, 1973, pp. 61–93, here pp. 64–67.

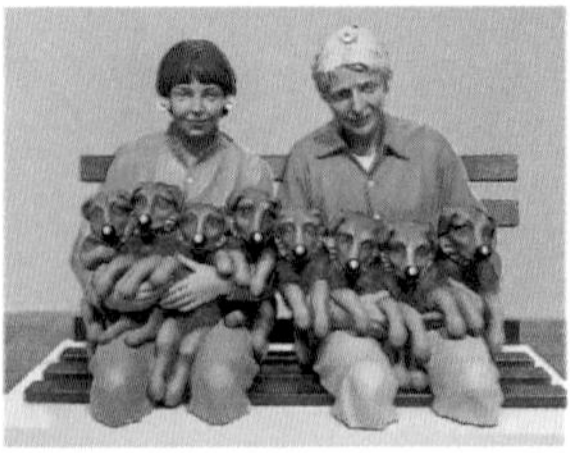

fig. 4

Jeff Koons,
String of Puppies, (Banality), 1988
Polychromed wood, 106.7 x 157.5 x 94 cm,
photo: John Wisniewski

By applying a variety of transparent, reflecting layers of colours – a procedure mainly developed by Jan van Eyck – it was possible to create a depth effect and a vital minuteness of detail. Linked to the mathematical principle of the central-perspective picture space, which imitates the natural visual perception, oil painting developed a realistic concept of representation. Its modern heritage can be found in photography and film, as forms of a chemical-industrially produced light painting, which now again reactivated natural light. Therefore photography was regarded as a sort of return of the icon.[4] Let me remind you of the portrait of Marlene Dietrich in this context. In line with this return or continuation of the sacral within industrial culture production and the myths of capitalist daily life, Walter Benjamin spoke of the 'gloss of divertissement.'

This gloss is the artistic theme of Jeff Koons. I think that his œuvre can be assigned to the critical perspective of Walter Benjamin since he, just like Benjamin, attempts a historically grounded interpretation of contemporary phenomena. And so Koons might imply a reference to the Arnolfini Wedding with his transformation of the photograph by Art Rogers titled Puppies into one of the sculptures of the *Banality* series [fig. 4], which made him famous at a stroke in 1988.

The little dog, a possession endowing pleasure and union to a couple, who present themselves in their happiness to us, went into serial reproduction 500 years later. The photograph's wit itself seems already informed by the avant-garde, as it works with Warhol's principle of seriality, combining the latter with the alluring charm of the puppy. Koons perverts this joke into a horrible kitschy object. In the picture's transformation into sculpture – a frequent Pygmalion-like method in Koons's œuvre – he implements an alienation [Verfremdung] concerning the status of the gloss: the natural light, transformed into spatial appearance by the photograph, is abolished and replaced. Instead a kind of anti-naturalistic middle-aged polychrome character marks the return of the sacral by means of a fetish-like objecthood. At the same time, the flat medium of the picture remains present due to the sculpture's fragmentation, which, nevertheless, no longer transports the meaning of the photograph as an extract from a larger whole. One could say that the ideological message of the photograph linked to the

---

4 See Hans Belting, *Bild und Kult: Eine Geschichte des Bildes vor dem Zeitalter der Kunst*, 2nd ed., Munich, 1991, p. 66.

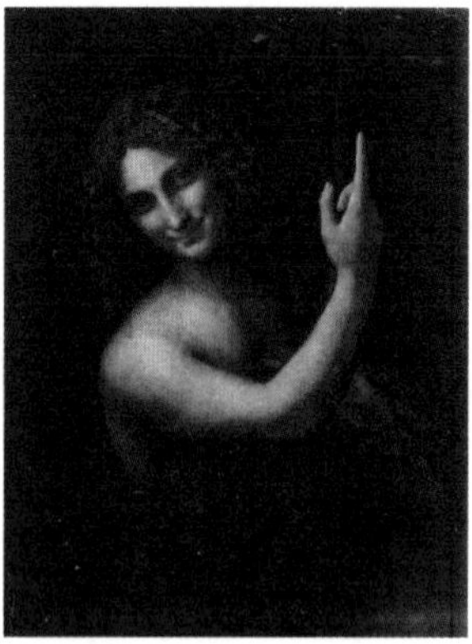

fig. 5

Leonardo,
St. John the Baptist,
1513–1516
Oil on canvas, 69 x 57 cm, Louvre, Paris

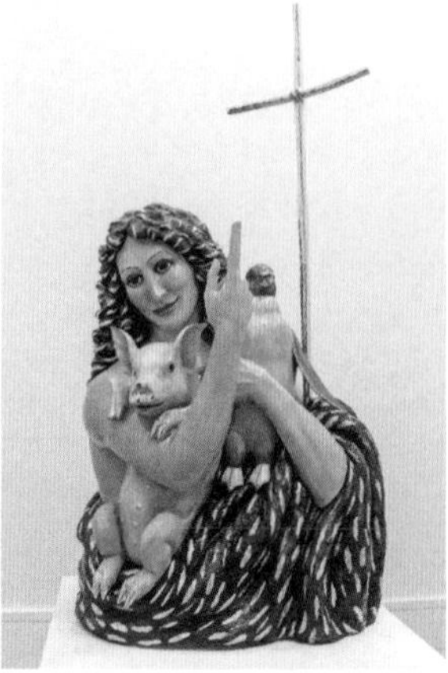

fig. 6

Jeff Koons,
St. John the Baptist
(Banality), 1988
Porcelain, 143.5 x 76.2 x 62.2 cm,
photo: Fred Romero on Flickr

Arnolfini Wedding, celebrating bourgeois life as a totality filled by love, is being torpedoed by the breaking and undermining of the respective genre laws.

At this point we are able to recognise Koons's most important artistic strategy: the negation of the logics of genre. He does so not in the sense of art's extension into life as proposed by Relational Aesthetics (Bourriaud) but by means of an art-immanent decisive negation (*bestimmte Negation*). In *Puppies* Koons reveals the fact that classic aesthetic totality and its promise of harmony and happiness is also at stake in the realm of popular culture and its witty appropriation of avant-garde aesthetics.[5] In *Puppies* he violently destroys this aesthetic totality by its sculptural reproduction, necessarily resulting in a fragment. At the same time, he pretends to heal the wound, to re-establish totality with an infantile-like gesture, which cites the childish nature of the romantic genius. By combining the animalistic, human and figural elements with the motive of the flowers, he represents again the desperate attempts to signify the wholeness of nature.

If this example does not perhaps illustrate the historical reference to early modern painting clear enough, the inspection of John the Baptist [fig. 5] will fully vindicate it. Concerning the treatment of light and the chiaroscuro, invented by himself, Leonardo pulls out all the stops in his masterpiece, culminating in the sfumato. A blurring of contours creates an atmospheric appearance of light and shade, which imparts an almost epiphany-like character to the pictorial world. This character is destroyed by Koons's sculpture St. John the Baptist [fig. 6] with sarcastic irony and the impression of a kitschy imitation. At first glance the sculpture looks like a monumental version of a souvenir object acquired in one of our contemporary museum shops. Again the grotesque abrogation of the pictorial and sculptural genres and the absurd commenting of the aesthetic totality by means of tender animal-human communities are at stake here. From the Baptist's right arm, which is pointed towards the sky as a sign of the Christian message of salvation sent

---

5 The most famous example, Koons remembers, is a surrealist ashtray: 'When I was a kid, my grandparents had an ashtray on a table in their television room. It was a small porcelain of a girl in a bathtub. It was white, with pink and blue details, and the legs went back and forth. As a kid, I was mesmerized. My Woman in Tub [1988] comes from that, though it also references Manet and Degas.' Jeff Koons, 'What Inspires Me Is Feeling', in *Art in America*, 18 June 2014 (http://www.artinamericamagazine.com/news-features/magazines/jeff-koons-muse/2018, accessed 9 June 2018).

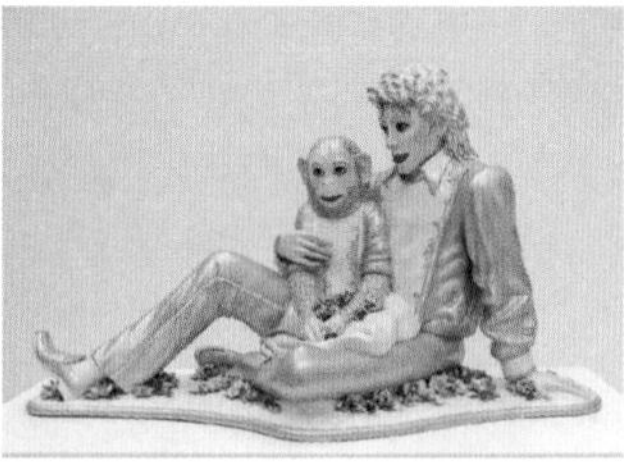

fig. 7

Jeff Koons,
'Michael Jackson and Bubbles',
(Banality), 1988
Porcelain, 106.7 x 179.1 x 82.6 cm,
photo: TinoM on Flickr

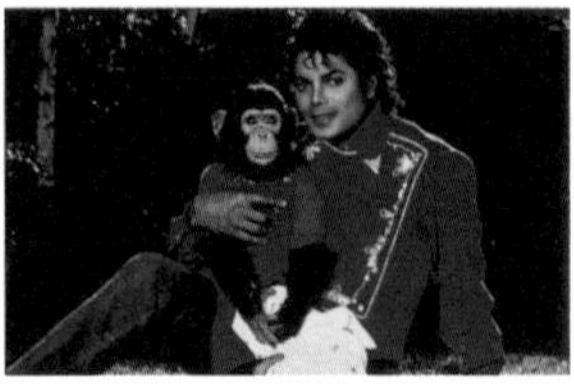

fig. 8

Michael Jackson and his chimp „Bubbles"

by God, a pig with golden trotters dangles. With his left arm, John holds a penguin. No lamb as far as the eye can see, which would have been at least acceptable as an animal companion of the Saint, can be found.

The golden gloss is again used literally here, inherent to the material itself, just like in the *Banality* series' most famous work Michael Jackson and Bubbles [fig. 7], which again is based on a photographic model [fig. 8]. Koons's sculpture shows the singer hugging his chimpanzee in an arrangement which connects Egyptian pathos with an aristocratic taste for exquisite porcelain. Hence Koons reinterprets the authenticity of the photographic light image as a fetish object, which links the gloss's promise of happiness completely to the preciousness of the material. This combination, as well, intentionally falls short of any plausibility. Both the monumental size and the subject itself oppose the Baroque centrepiece, which is invoked by form and material. And the elaborated surface of porcelain negates the monumental ambition.

The uneasy feelings in regard to Koons's *Banality* works, voiced at the time by critics, are probably also comprehensible when looking at the life-size wood sculpture Buster Keaton, modelled by Koons after a still image from the movie Our Hospitality (1923). With the figures of the singer, the saint and the film star, Koons ultimately deals with the trans-individual figure of the artist, which, according to the Romantic tradition, is endowed with an intimate connection to the non-human nature. Koons articulates the truth of the cultural-industrial celebration of self-alienation, of which Benjamin speaks as the already cited 'gloss of divertissement.' The latter is only penetrable if the aesthetic appearance of the gloss is attacked and staged as the return of an archaic material fetishism.

In this respect I would argue that Koons starts a rebellion against the aesthetic semblance, even though, more than any other artist, he seems to be addicted to it. My theoretical parameters are both Benjamin's argument of the modern decline of the aura and, connected to the latter, Adorno's aesthetic theory, which dialectically links the rebellion against the aesthetic semblance with the necessity of its redemption. For only by holding on to artistic autonomy, the treacherous glamour of cultural-industrial productions can be perforated and denounced as regression to barbarism.

The glamour of mass media's photographic and filmic image productions in general celebrates no longer a transcendental divine authority but the quasi-religious cult of capitalism, as the star icon

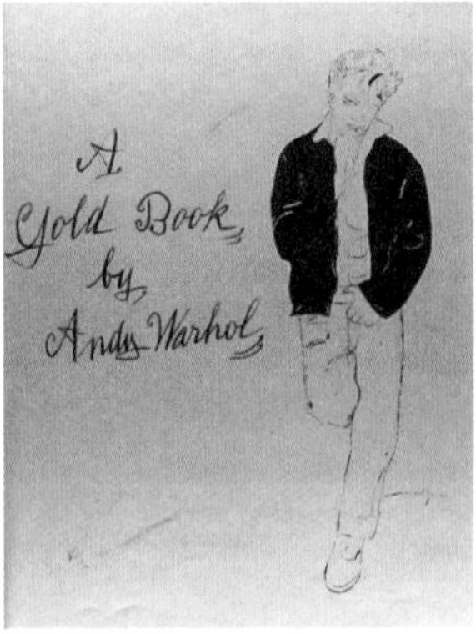

fig. 9

Andy Warhol,
Gold Book, 1957
The Andy Warhol Foundation for the Visual Arts, Artists Rights Society, New York

shows.[6] The reign of the exchange value is the logic of this cult, which does not offer any other redemption than the permanent joining in its rituals, the participation in the chain of exploitation. The commodity stages itself in a neo-feudal manner, by means of its aesthetic surfaces and packaging, particularly with the gloss of metallic or transparent foils[7] carrying on the promise of immortality beyond any religious orthodoxy while the fictional space of the promise has now become total.

Celebration: Koons after Pop Art

The traditional meaning of the shine, the glitter and glare derived from the aesthetics of advertisement – the symbolical gift of an Elysian life – is reflected in Koons's artistic work and specifically called upon in the title of his series *Celebration*, to which I will turn to in the following. It deals with the transcending of daily life in the celebration, which is traditionally affirmed by presents and jewellery. Starting in 1994 the group of works treated sculptures and paintings as equals for the first time, sometimes using identical objects, with a repertoire in motives ranging from toys, flowers, jewellery and decorative objects of various kinds. In all these motives the holiday-like exaggeration of existence is at stake and, thus, indirectly, art itself, too. To say it as Friedrich Schiller did: the 'Joy, beautiful spark of the Gods' is mirrored and also demolished in Koons's shiny objects and pictures, keeping in mind the sense of the other within the bourgeois, rationalised way of living. The large-scale paintings of the series present objects almost always on high-gloss crinkled foils, which infinitely reflect the motive. Different to his predecessors Andy Warhol and especially Gerhard Richter, whose main theme is the painterly illusion of luster, Koons exaggerates the false nimbus of the high-gloss surfaces. He adopts the method of painting after

---

6 Walter Benjamin, 'Kapitalismus als Religion' (1921), in *Gesammelte Schriften*, vol. VI: *Fragmente, Autobiographische Schriften*, Frankfurt am Main, 1991, pp. 100–3. Regine Prange, '*"Taufe im Mainstream"? – Über die Kunst von Jeff Koons, mit Walter Benjamin betrachtet*', in Toni Hildebrandt (ed.), *Kunst und Kirche: Ökumenische Zeitschrift für zeitgenössische Kunst und Architektur*, vol. 1/2017: *Profanierungen*, Wien, 2017, pp. 28–33. The full text of this article was published at http://archiv.ub.uni-heidelberg.de/artdok/volltexte/2017/5244, accessed 30 July 2018.

7 See the remark on foils by Wolfgang Fritz Haug, *Kritik der Warenästhetik: Überarbeitete Neuausgabe: Gefolgt von Warenästhetik im High-Tech-Kapitalismus*, Frankfurt am Main, 2009, p. 79, n. 8.

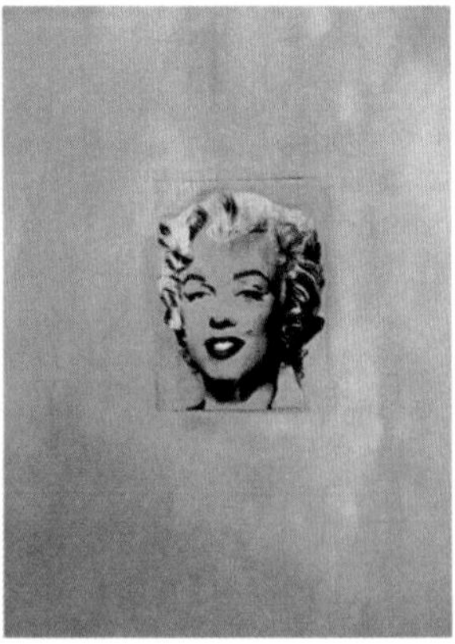

fig. 10

Andy Warhol,
Gold Marilyn Monroe, 1962

Silkscreen on acryl and oil on canvas, 211.4 x 144.7 cm, The Andy Warhol Foundation for the Visual Arts, Artists Rights Society, New York

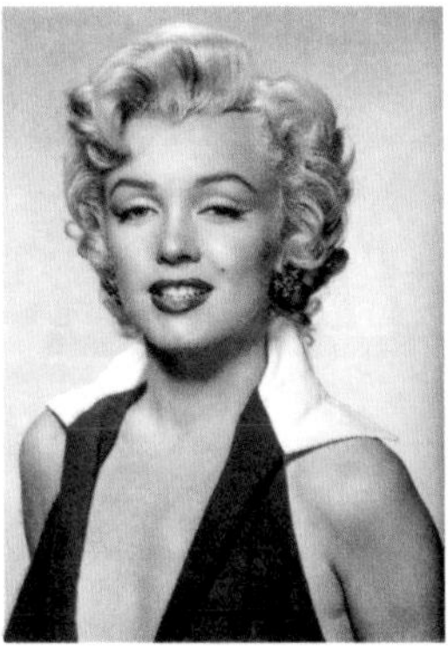

fig. 11

Marilyn Monroe

photographs, but instead of the painterly sfumato, he chooses a kind of digital realism.

As associated with the names Warhol and Richter, Koons is not the first artist who made the transition of the aesthetic semblance to the products of the consumer society his artistic subject. He mainly refers to Warhol, who, in his days as a commercial artist, reactivated the Byzantine golden background – as an enamel foil for his modernist-laconic blotted line – in drawings commissioned by a manufacturer of shoes. In Golden Boy fig. 9 the masculine nonchalance of the posing young man in his bomber jacket is composed after Edward Wallowitch's photograph Young Man Smoking a Cigarette (ca. 1956), the subject of which is posing like James Dean, hence anticipating the involvement with the star icon by the avant-garde artist Andy Warhol, which Jeff Koons continued in his own way, as we have seen in Michael Jackson and Bubbles fig. 7. Golden Marilyn fig. 10, one of Warhol's first star portraits, reveals, in contrast to the elegant advertising images, its character as a collage. It can also be interpreted as a historical construction in the sense of Benjamin's dialectical picture.[8] The contemporary portrait of Marilyn Monroe, the erotic ideal of the 1950s, is connected to its historical original, the divine queen Mary. Marilyn Monroe's sex appeal becomes readable as a memory and attempted fulfilment of a much more comprehensive divine love. Yet Warhol does not attempt to simulate gloss and preciousness, which is another difference to his commercial images. The portrait, placed on a separated golden plane, is clearly applied and looks strange in the golden surroundings, with its artificial, stark colours. The colour of the hair, make-up and eyeshadow remain recognisable as means of production of the star's face, while in the photograph – a publicity still fig. 11, which serves as a model – those means of production have vanished behind the shining, quasi-natural appearance. By revealing, so to speak, the paint box, Warhol presents himself as a successor of the Abstract Expressionists and Rauschenberg's Proto-Pop. The painterly gesture of Art Informel is actually lifted to a new level, filtered by

---

8 I refer to the conception Benjamin points out in his *Theses on History*. Walter Benjamin, 'Über den Begriff der Geschichte', in *Gesammelte Schriften*, vol. I/1. Suhrkamp Verlag, Frankfurt am Main 1991: *Abhandlungen*, pp. 691–704, especially p. 701 (XIX). Benjamin's materialistic notion of history is not far away from the aesthetics of montage: 'Die Geschichte ist Gegenstand einer Konstruktion, deren Ort nicht die homogene und leere Zeit, sondern die von Jetztzeit erfüllte bildet. […] Sie ist der Tigersprung ins Vergangene.'

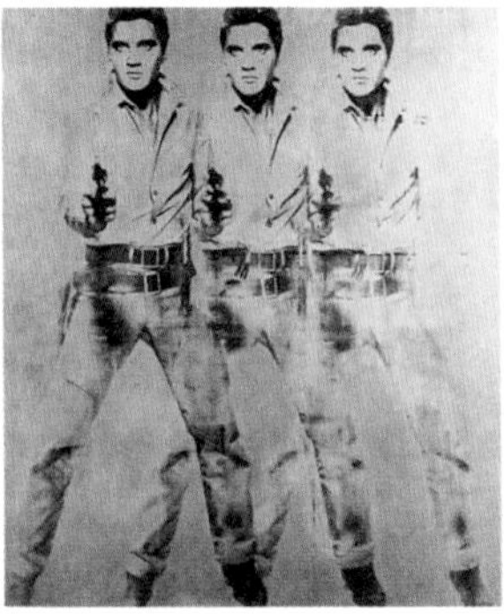

fig. 12

Andy Warhol,
Triple Elvis, 1962

Silver paint, spray paint and silkscreen ink on canvas, The Andy Warhol Foundation for the Visual Arts, Artists Rights Society, New York the technical image of the mass media. So it is not by accident that the subject of the gloss continues in Warhol's work mostly in the form of the silver colour and foil, which particularly fulfil the commercial and technological dimension of the aesthetic semblance. Warhol quotes the shimmering television or cinematographic screen by using the colour silver. His studio "The Factory" is coated with tinfoil to that effect. Triple Elvis fig. 12 appears as a media star on a silver background. However, silver is also the colour of money, as Warhol's painting One Dollar Bill (Silver Certificate) (1962) illustrates.

By means of an obvious repetition, Jeff Koons's Triple Elvis – from the series Popeye makes for a tribute but also a rejection of Warhol's strategies. The hyperrealism of the photographic image, here in the figure of the pin-up girl appearing in three different positions and an inflatable toy lobster placed across them, is manifested with all its illusionist blaze of light, be it the skin or the plastic surface. In Warhol's work the photographic realism is deprived of its effect by the transformation into a modernist style of flatness. And still seriality and montage as Warholian methods are still valid and effectual, even if a reverse direction is now being pursued. Koons torpedoes the beautiful semblance by his grotesque exaggeration and an excessive multiplication which bursts the aesthetic boundaries. He does not employ trash aesthetics and linear scarcity, Warhol's subtle shabby look. But one could even discover an iconographic paraphrase of the androgyny of the hero Elvis Presley in his part as a 'half-blood' in the movie Flaming Star, which Warhol chose as a model for Triple Elvis. The lobster in Koons's Triple Elvis, borrowed from Salvador Dalí's erotic pictorial world, is, after all, a clearly bisexual motive.

For the series *Celebration*, the tradition of Pop Art is of decisive significance. Their protagonists already discovered the opportunity to reveal the methods of classical painting and sculpture within the popular pictorial worlds of cinema, magazines and advertising as well as in the shape of commodities themselves. Within this field of an aesthetic capitalism, they continued a modernist self-critique of art, the attack to classical beauty.[9] What comes to the fore, hence, is Horkheimer's and Adorno's analysis of the culture industry, which

9 Regine Prange, 'Roy Lichtensteins "Yellow and Green Brushstrokes" (1966): Die Revision der Meisterhand', in Reinhard Brandt (ed.), *Meisterwerke der Malerei*, Leipzig, 2001, pp. 247–87, and *Das Schöne in der Gesellschaft des Spektakels: Zu Warhols Lonesome Cowboys* (1968), available at http://archiv.ub.uni-heidelberg.de/artdok/volltexte/2017/5122, accessed 30 July 2018.

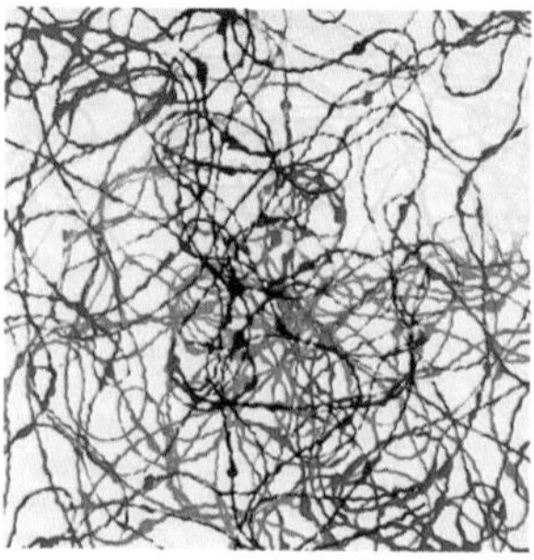

fig. 13

Andy Warhol,
Yarn Series, 1983

Acrylic paint and silkscreen on canvas, 102 x 102 cm, The Andy Warhol Foundation for the Visual Arts, Artists Rights Society, New York supposedly hands out the heritage of art to the masses in a democratic manner. Seemingly rendering accessible the gift of experiencing and producing art to each and every consumer, the culture industry according to Horkheimer and Adorno actually leads to stultification, even to new barbarism. Warhol, similar to Koons, processed this industrial-cultural production, which does not serve liberty but the capital instead, in a no less critical manner. Just like Adorno postulates in his *Aesthetic Theory*,[10] both artists position art's autonomy directly against the totality of the semblance in the culture industry, by revealing art's immanence through their alienations of the product image.

Hence Warhol's Yarn series [fig. 13] and Koons's Ribbon can be understood as a continuation of Pollock's Drip Painting with different means.[11] Perhaps one could speak of a cultural-industrial disguise of the avant-gardist impetus. The ribbon, maybe also combined with a gift tag in the shape of a heart as Koons has formed it in his monumental Hanging Heart, is a modest and omnipresent nimbus, which democratises the promise beyond religious beliefs, linking it solely to the exchange of goods. In *Celebration* Koons deals with the phenomenon that the exchange of presents is staged ('celebrated') as a fair exchange giving the impression of escaping economic conditions.[12] In fact, however, the logic of the commodity fetish finds its confirmation here. The staging of the commodity in itself serves the promise of a special use value, an increased vital experience of living, which replaced the hope on resurrection, at least in the rich industrialised societies. Koons reminds us of these ideological transformations by means of isolating the iconography of Christ's Sacred Heart.[13] The claim that salvation depends on

---

10 Theodor W. Adorno, *Aesthetic Theory* (1970), ed. Gretel Adorno and Rolf Tiedemann, newly translated, edited, and with a translator's introduction by Robert Hullot-Kentor, London/New York, 1997. Certainly to employ Adorno's notion of the artwork means also to desist his objection to late modern art.

11 It is worth noting here that Pollock was already using the cheap thrill of aluminium paint in many of his drip paintings.

12 The basic ethnological research on this topic was made by Marcel Mauss in his 'Essai sur le don' (1923/24).

13 To stress the Christian hope of salvation, a sculpture named Sacred Heart is part of the *Celebration* series. An accumulation of the popular heart motive already takes place on the surface and the surroundings of *Amore* (1988, Museum Brandhorst, Munich), which belongs to the *Banality* series. On Christian iconography and the central theme of salvation in Koons's œuvre, see Raphael Bouvier, *Jeff Koons: Der Künstler als Täufer*, Munich, 2012. I do not agree, though, with the author's

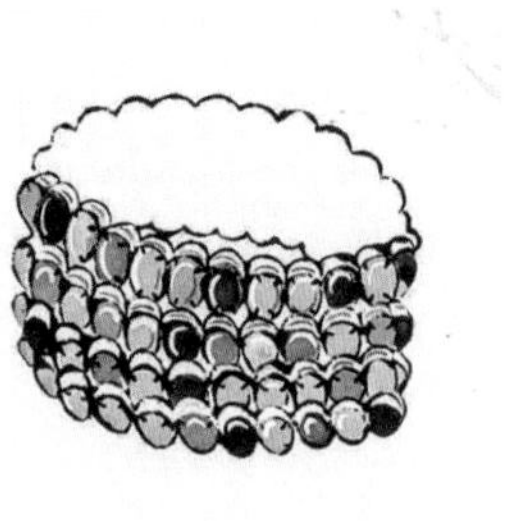

fig. 14

Andy Warhol,
Bracelet, 1955

Ink and tempera on firm pape, 20.8 x 23.8 cm, The Andy Warhol Foundation for the Visual Arts, Artists Rights Society, New York

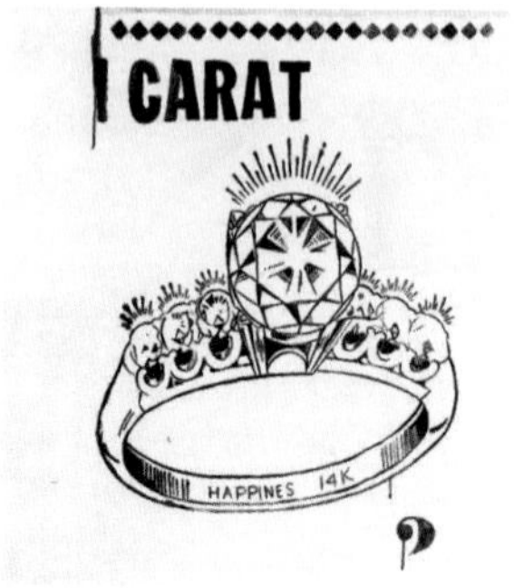

fig. 15

Andy Warhol,
Carat, 1961

Water based paint on canvas, 132.7 x 121.9 cm, The Andy Warhol Foundation for the Visual Arts, Artists Rights Society, New York passion, that the joy of consumption might also mean death, hence that the promise of love is ambivalent, is articulated explicitly by Koons in several interviews: the *Celebration* sculpture *Cat on a Clothesline (Blue Sock)* (1994–2001), after a postcard illustration, originated from the idea to create 'an interesting kind of crucifixion'.[14] *Bracelet* fig. 14 looks like a crown of thorns, but it could also be a present.[15] The same uncertainty is already expressed in *Amore* (1988), a teddy bear in porcelain, which anticipates the toy motive and the subject of the gift in *Celebration*: 'you don't know if Amore loves you – because it holds a little "I love you" badge – or whether it wants to be loved.'[16] The teddy's extended arms as well as the artist's extremely cheerful posing, 'offering' his artwork to the public , evokes the image of the crucifixion.

Let's keep in mind here that the gift as a celebration of life signifies the emancipated idea of art against the false gift of the commodity and its ideology of participation. With the exemplary motive of the engagement ring, we can observe how Warhol derives the motive from his commercial art production and endows it with the said reflections on the connection between product and fortune in his 1961 painting *Carat* fig. 15. The latter is actually a painterly imitation of an advertisement for a particularly inexpensive diamond ring.[17] The supposed diamond is, beyond any spatial logic, suggestively moved closer towards the spectator. Just like each of the little stones at its sides, the diamond is equipped with an aureole, reminding one of the style of comics, illustrating the sign-like coagulation of the sacral motive in the ring ad. Of a similar importance is, besides the information '14 carat' (gold), the word 'Happines' in the gravure on the ring's inner side, which Warhol spelt incorrectly

---

interpretation, which fails to recognise the dialectical and critical argumentation of the artist, who does not at all give us a programme for salvation, as Bouvier postulates.

14 '"There Is No Art in It". Isabelle Graw in Conversation with Jeff Koons', in *Jeff Koons The Painter and Sculptor*, ed. Matthias Ulrich, Vinzenz Brinkmann, Joachim Pissarro and Max Hollein, exh. cat. Schirn Kunsthalle Frankfurt am Main and Liebieghaus Skulpturensammlung, Ostfildern, 2012, pp. 75–83, here p. 80.

15 Theodora Vischer, 'Dialoge der Selbstakzeptanz: Jeff Koons erzählt über sich und sein Werk: Aus Gesprächen mit dem Künstler, New York, Februar 2012, Teil 1', in Jeff Koons, ed. Fondation Beyeler, Basel/Theodora Vischer, Hatje Cantz, 2012, pp. 11–36, here p. 34.

16 Graw, 'There Is No Art in It' (note 14), p. 77.

17 Anthony E. Grudin, 'Mythos und Klasse in Warhols frühen Zeitungsbildern', in *Warhol: Headlines*, exh. cat. Museum für Moderne Kunst, Frankfurt am Main, 2012, pp. 36–47, here p. 47, ill. 15.

on purpose. It is missing an 's', which leads to the impression that this 's' needs to be added, in order for happiness to be complete. The ring advertisement was published in tabloid newspapers such as the *New York Daily News*, read by blue-collar workers, an economically disadvantaged customer base, which was courted with particularly cheap and seemingly still luxurious products. Warhol revealed the promise of cultural participation, which is linked to consumerism. In our example it is the performative imitation of a class living in luxury.

How strongly Koons followed Warhol's example can be illustrated on the basis of his own artistic analysis of class-specific logics of advertisement in *Luxury and Degradation* (1986). I would like to name only one striking feature since it leads us onto the tracks of a critical distancing from Warhol. While the latter transforms the pictorial language of advertisement into a personal handwriting, despite all fragility and material meagreness, the sculptor Koons refuses the credo of graphic authorship and returns to the radical origin of the ready-made. The alcohol advertisements, a whole series of glossy advertising posters that Koons reproduces exactly by oil prints on canvas, are shown without any changes to the motive. And the ready-mades created by Koons himself do not attempt to alloy with modernist aesthetics of abstraction. Rather they enforce the products in their physically tangible yet, due to their gloss, seemingly intangible concreteness.

Let us now look at the reference to Warhol in *Celebration*. Koons creates an equivalence between the various kinds of commodities, while the gloss of the mirror mostly replaces the equalising principle of Warhol's seriality, which dissolves the gestalt. His oil paintings after photographs, e.g. *Cake* (1995–97), *Bread with Egg* (1995–97), *Plate Set* (1995–98) and *Bracelet* [fig. 14], show objects of one and the same cheap league of products.

Similar to Warhol, Koons also aims at the do-it-yourself culture.[18] He presents the material Play-Doh and Colouring Book as products as well as possible presents, which prove to be means of production for infantile artistry, a material fit for practicing the consumerist participation in culture. Koons compares his method, to transform the photographic model into an oil painting by

18 See e.g. Andy Warhol, *Do It Yourself (Flowers)*, 1962, *Do It Yourself (Narcissus)*, ca. 1962, and *Do It Yourself (Seascape)*, 1962, in *Andy Warhol: The Early Sixties: Gemälde und Zeichnungen 1961–1964*, exh. cat. Kunstmuseum Basel, Ostfildern, 2010, pp. 90–5, cat. nos 9–11.

means of a simplifying clarification, with the method of painting by numbers practiced as a child.[19]

The series of the monumental *Diamond* represents this generalisation of the aesthetic by the culture industry. *Diamond* is created in five colour versions, like a mass-produced T-shirt which serves the desire of individuality. The *Diamond* sculptures do not emanate any other significance than the monumental gift tag in the form of a heart or the huge semi-abstract Elephant (1994–97). Koons's *Diamond* might be derived directly from the early Warhol painting *Carat* fig. 15, as he seems to translate its perspective representation into literal three-dimensionality. Koons continues and enforces the process of isolating and enlarging the motive of the newspaper's ad. He even isolates the stone with its frame, so there is no ring to be worn by a finger! The sculpture unifies – and that is why it still might be programmatic for the series – the non-organic nature of the edged facets with an organic, plump-looking formation of the frame, which seems to hold the stone with what looks like fleshy claw arms. In contrast to this symbolic gluing of the dead and the living into a kind of cosmic metaphor, the form of this work is a fragment, which makes it different from most of the other works which depict complete objects and thus use values. Significantly *Colouring Book* is also not shown as a complete object. Yet the fragment has been designed with the same perfection and shining surface as all the other trivial things.

Here we are confronted with the dissent. Koons lets us know by means of his insistent technological perfectionism that Warhol did not escape from the gestalt of the commodity in his masterly graphic appropriation and aesthetic transformation of the trivial. It seems meaningful to me that until now Koons did not produce a painterly version of *Diamond* or of *Colouring Book*, as if the sense of these works of art could only be mediated by sculptures, oppositional answers to Warhol's pictorial flatness and the sensitive and subtle trash character of his art. Maybe Koons's dialogue with Warhol can be compared with the dialogue between Barnett Newman and Piet Mondrian. Like Newman he raises the quality of the sublime. With his overwhelming formats and drastic shiny

---

19 The relationship between Koons's painting techniques and Warhol's *Do It Yourself* series is mentioned by Raphael Bouvier, 'Jeff Koons' Serien *The New, Banality* und *Celebration*: drei Marksteine einer Entwicklung', in *Jeff Koons* (note 13), pp. 173–89, here p. 186.

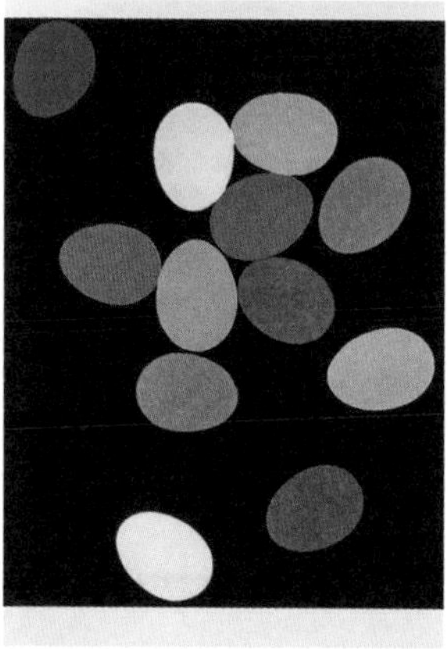

fig. 16

Andy Warhol,
Egg Painting, 1982

Silkscreen paint and acrylic on canvas, 229 x 178 cm, The Andy Warhol Foundation for the Visual Arts, Artists Rights Society, New York

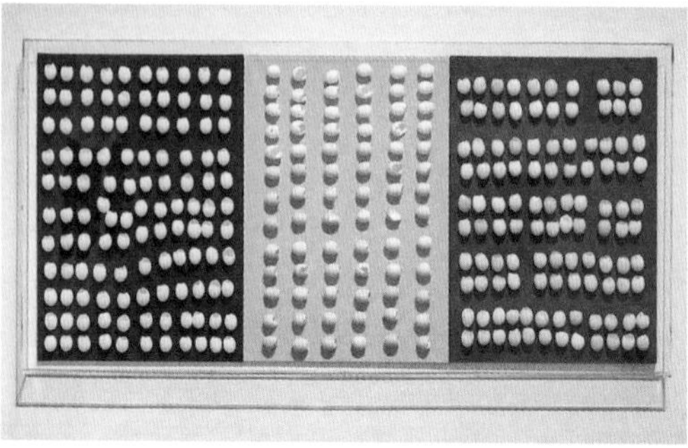

fig. 17

Marcel Broodthaers,
Untitled (Triptych), 1965–1966

Eggshells on painted canvas
© VG Bild-Kunst, Bonn 2020

volumes, Koons creates a moment of absolute presence, a violent attack against the aesthetic boundary.[20]

Another work – *Cracked Egg* – does not fit into the ensemble of the *Celebration* objects, since it fulfils the characteristics of neither a gift article nor a toy, nor a decorative object, which one could buy in a shop. This work, as well, can be understood as a quote. Warhol's œuvre, however, is only the weaker of two references, namely his late *Egg Paintings* fig. 16, which, based on a decorative Easter motive, use the form of the egg as a module of a kind of colour field painting. Here again Warhol transforms the three-dimensional into a two-dimensional, highly subtle composition, which is fertilised by the hard-edge aesthetics of post painterly abstraction. The egg, a natural symbol of a unified form holding life, has been used up by the planar colour in Warhol's painting, damaged by the clashing contours. Koons chooses another form of violation of this ideal form, namely the depiction of an actual fracture, the egg being broken in two halves, as if a chick had already hatched out. However, the chromed steel does not hint at a living creature, from the outside or the inside. The reification has become total.

Koons highlights this character also in contrast to the second, closer artist of reference, Marcel Broodthaers, who worked with real egg shells multiple times fig. 17. Aside from clams they are, as it were, the remnants of a typical Belgian meal, pictorialised or transformed into a broken ready-made sculpture by Broodthaers, who thus modifies the material collages of Kurt Schwitters. Being a protagonist of Concept Art, Broodthaers plays an ironic game with the formats and methods of art as with the art business in general. His affection for kitschy objects, which he collected for his Eagle Museum, is widely known. Without a doubt his work, using art as a critical means, has inspired Koons. Yet I would like to underline that he takes on a position which differs from both Pop Art and Concept Art without forsaking their achievements: the reflection on art and its relation to the culture industry. Koons, however, rejects not only the aestheticisation of trash in Warhol but also the anarchical refusal of the artwork in Broodthaers. With Adorno he shares the insight that true art needs to rebel against its character

20 'It is as if the elation of the surprise knew no boundaries, and even the social differences among viewers were suspended for an instant.' Achim Hochdörfer, 'The Gift of Art', in Scott Rothkopf (ed.), *Jeff Koons: A Retrospective*, exh. cat. Whitney Museum of American Art, New York, New Haven/London, 2014, here p. 237.

of semblance yet simultaneously needs to save it as the decisive means of resilience against social reality.[21]

The industrial perfection of *Cracked Egg* is a slap in the face for a subversive non-conformity, which, also in the case of Concept Art, still prefers the esprit and wit of the individual artist over any material realisation of an idea. Contrarily (and paradoxically) Koons stresses that art stems from savvy, even though he does not execute the technical production by himself. Sketches and preparatory drawings by the artist are not known to the public. Anyway we trust him saying that he does not want to disappoint any expectations of a perfect realisation and thus does not allow himself the smallest imperfect detail when producing his objects. They are planned and prepared over a long period of time. Special procedures had to be developed in order to meet the formal idea of Koons. In some cases, it is said, about 15,000 hours of work were spent on such sculptures.[22]

With this appropriation of industrial materials and industrial production, Koons refers to a third artistic tradition of the 1960s: the Minimalism of Donald Judd. However, he does not follow him when it comes to the purism of the abstract form. Koons's position towards his artistic predecessors can be understood as a culmination of the critique of authorship they had already postulated. *Cracked Egg* immobilises, so to speak, the iconoclastic gesture of Marcel Broodthaers and also Judd's abstraction in a product-like, reified gestalt.

This dialectics of the gloss can also be observed in the photographic montage with the lettering 'Critically Gone'. The criticality of the avant-gardes has passed, since their gestures of destruction have been crystallised into an aureole of glass, as the photographic composition illustrates. In other words: the avant-garde iconoclasm has become part of the spectacle and can only be called up and preserved in this alienated form.[23]

Koons's art is missing the playful character of Dadaism and its followers as well as the hermetic sternness of abstraction. Both methods are refused by him as artists' inconsequential attempts to

---

21 On the crises and the redemption of semblance, see Adorno, *Aesthetic Theory* (note 10), pp. 100–7.

22 Koons's coloured high-grade steel sculptures were, by the way, produced in a classical metalworking business, the Arnold AG in Friedrichsdorf, Hessen (Germany).

23 For a detailed comment and illustration of this publication, see Prange, 'Taufe im Mainstream?' (note 6).

secure an autonomy beyond the capitalist reality. And yet it is by affirmation of the commodity fetish that he develops a re-erection of the category of the work of art. The way he does that, namely by a discursive interlocking of objects and tableaux within the compound of a series, can best be explained by a Conceptualist approach. The model of Marcel Broodthaers is important in regard to the merging of material and artistic work with the sphere of education and reception. The complete apparatus of the art as institution becomes a part of art itself. That's why Koons defines himself and can be seen as a Concept artist. Curatorial stagings in historical rooms or museum collections and also his personal commentaries including photographic poses in and with his artworks draw no less attention than the objects and works themselves, and justifiably so.

Art as theory as art. Koons's critique of semblance

The artist's statements in interviews, lectures and essays, accompanying his artistic production since the late 1980s, offer further starting points for exploring the dialectics of the gloss in *Celebration*. Particularly the interview as a form which aims at explaining the artist's intentions and biographical background in order to give sense to the work is no less parodied by Koons than are all the artistic formats with which he works as a painter and sculptor. The irony of the published talks with Koons lies within the fact that his interview partners do not see through his rhetoric habitus, understanding the contents of question and answer in a literal sense and thus fully live in their role, a role which is perceived by Koons to be a sculptural material, beyond any immediacy. Interviews with Koons hence should be understood as critical artworks, with the interviewer personifying the space of the art exhibition with all its ideological implications and Koons, with his answers, absolving a performance which presents, as do all his works, the humanistic disguise of consumerist democracy.[24] Simultaneously, his interview

24 First detailed analyses about Koons' interviews have been presented by Anne Breucha, *Die Kunst der Postproduktion. Jeff Koons in seinen Interviews*, Munich: Wilhelm Fink, 2014. Breucha rightly claims, that the interviews are part of Koons' œuvre. But as she does not introduce a theory of art and history, Koons' statements could be related to a convincing interpretation that is not yet graspable. In the end, she makes out two possible ways to understand Koons' activities: either he can be seen as defender of his ideal of equality, or he can be seen as a very

performance, with a seemingly nonchalant rhetoric, is fragmented, calls upon the traditions of a critical aesthetics of montage.

The interview with Peter-Klaus Schuster, which took place in 2008 at an exhibition of the *Celebration* series at the Neue Nationalgalerie in Berlin, allows us to substantiate this evaluation. On the series' genesis, Koons explains as followed:

"The *Celebration* series is based on a calendar year. I started this photo shoot for a catalogue for Anthony d'Offay [a British art dealer, R.P.]. Then I realized it was too good [...]. There is a sense of a calendar here – like *Tulips* representing spring and *Cat on a Clothesline* could be like Easter. With *Hanging Heart*, or *Sacred Heart*, there are these different aspects of kind of a year. Some are not so specific, but there is a sense of the cyclical."[25]

It is odd that Koons assigns *Cat on a Clothesline* (1994–2001), which links domestic happiness with a cute pet, to Easter and does not, which would be more obvious, mention *Cracked Egg* or the gigantic *Baroque Egg with Bow (Turquoise / Magenta)*, (1994–2008), which was also exhibited in Berlin, or the likewise exhibited *Bowl with Eggs (Green)* (1994–2008). It remained unclear in the interview why the motive of the heart could be referring to a certain season or a certain holiday.

Apparently confused by this non-clarity, Schuster asks 'It's celebrating the year, the highlights of the year?' Following socio-historic premises of art-historian research, he seems to aim at reconstructing the sense of the series through the idea of a photo calendar.

Koons does not specifically confirm this but instead introduces the universal idea of memory, which is linked with the pleasant prospect of a happy future: 'Time, the sense of time, a sense of remembrance, but also things that you look forward to.'[26]

Asked about the childlike aspect of being given a present, he continues: "Receiving and giving I really think is an important dialogue, at least with the floral sculptures and the Baroque-type references. There was always this dialogue of serving and being served, all the types of polarities in the Baroque. Also with my own

---

successful and strategic entrepreneur.

25 Peter-Klaus Schuster in Conversation with Jeff Koons, in: Anette Hüsch (ed.), *Jeff Koons: Celebration*. Neue Nationalgalerie Berlin, Ostfildern, 2008, pp. 82-93, here p. 93.

26 Ibid.

children, they ask about their birthdays, their birthdays could be ten months off, but they'll say: 'Dad, please, can I have this for my birthday?' But also they can look back and say: 'The cake Mom made for my birthday, boy that was great! It was in the shape of a dinosaur.' It's this sense of past, future and present."[27]

It is remarkable here how Koons talks about the awareness of history as a general theme of his work, how he, reaching beyond the occasion of the calendar order and the reminiscence of the Christian year, defines history as a story of exchange, of giving and taking. He is in fact interested neither in the celebration of anthropological laws nor in the redemptive liberation of the discriminating border between art and kitsch, between real and commercial art. The propaganda of acceptance, as the speaker of which Koons appears, is actually the propaganda of the commodity and its inherent aesthetics. By bringing this up and visualising it, Koons plays commodity's melody to itself, in order to break its power. The 'theological spleens' of the commodity, as described by Marx,[28] are demonstrated by Koons in the excess of the empty gloss and the cold glow, for the sake of their clarification.

His first series of works, *The New*, in which he, at first without success, invested his accumulated capital, identifies the necessity of innovation of commodity production and visualises the numinous promise of fortune connected to it. Koons presented a variety of brand new, modernistically designed vacuum cleaners, the polished surfaces of which are endowed with a sacral aura in spotlighted vitrines which look like shrines, a reference to the Minimalist light art of Dan Flavin. The said theological moment of the commodity has been a subject of Jeff Koons from the beginning.

I follow Scott Rothkopf in his argument stating that Koons, when he was working as a stock broker in those early days, did not really develop a mercantile talent but subordinated these activities to his art.[29] His competing with capital-intensive industrial production and with the workshops of popular-cultural spheres needs to be understood as an artistic method, a continuation of the criticism

---

27 Ibid.

28 Karl Marx, *Capital* (*Das Kapital*, 1867), Part I, Chapter 1, Section 4: 'The Fetishism of Commodities and the Secret Thereof'. According to Marx the mystical character of commodities originates in the determining factors of value.

29 Scott Rothkopf, 'No Limits', in Rothkopf, *Jeff Koons: A Retrospective* (footnote 20), pp. 15–35, here p. 27.

of the utopianism and individualism of modernist concepts of art. The era of socialist visions of a juster society, led on by art, had ended after World War II, when the force of absorption of the big industries could not be ignored anymore, when Jackson Pollock became a media star and his radical abstraction was demeaned into a setting for fashion photography. As mentioned before, Koons, even more than Andy Warhol and his generation, realises that art can no longer just stand next to society and claim its difference but has to take account of the fact that it is part of the apparatus of utilisation and can thus only speak from the inside of the capitalist conditions.

It is necessary to read Koons's statements very closely in order to discover their quite oppositional philosophical sense, since on the surface of his comments, he presents himself as a naive apostle of a gospel of acceptance, within which many believed to discover a refusal of the critical culture of the avant-gardes and neo-avant-gardes, a saviour finally burying the strict expectations of good taste. I already mentioned that the dictum 'Critically Gone' in a programmatic photographic montage for Artforum has an ambivalent sense, not only due to the visually present, iconoclastic, extremely 'critical' deed which contradicts the text. Within the series of photographs and especially in regard to the adjacent one, which combines the interior of St. Paul's Chapel in New York with the slogan 'Liberated Mainstream', it generates another meaning. Looking at the spread pages rather allows a reversal of the statement, which then reads 'Liberated (/) critically' – 'Mainstream (/) Gone'.

In the more recent interview text, Koons has let us know that he is working on the story of exchange, of giving and taking, connecting this with the cognitive activities of remembering and desiring. Mom's cake in the form of a dinosaur may stand as a metaphor for Koons's own art, which employs the kitsch object to start a leap forward (Tigersprung) into the past, in the sense that it has been defined by Benjamin as the work of the materialistic historian[30].

30 See note 8.

The darker side. *Balloon Dog* as the Trojan horse

A second anecdote concerning the *Celebration* series introduces a dark side to the gift which both the commodity and art pretend to be. Koons narrates both anecdotes as an answer to the Romantic assumption of him worshipping an infantile creativity. I quote Schuster: 'Somehow with Celebration I have the feeling that you look at the world of children with the child as creator.'[31]

Koons replies to the question with a striking distinction between his personal, vital preferences and his art. This differentiation is apparently far from the art-historical fixation on the artist subject. Koons ostensibly serves this craving for the artist novel again and again, yet at this point he specifically separates his personally experienced enjoyment of the here and now, which Schuster believes to have found in his work, from an also tragic sense within his art: 'I like to embrace things. Breathing, lying on the ground, and smelling the grass. Just enjoying that smell and color.'

Without any transition the now quoted sentence follows: 'Somehow, Celebration does have a darker side to it. [...] Even though the outside could be joyous, the inside was a little dark. It's like the *Balloon Dog* having this very joyous outside, but at the same time an equestrian, Trojan-horse quality. You could feel presence of the inside.'

The Trojan horse was offered as a gift to the citizens of Troy in a sanctimoniously intention by the Greeks, only serving as a vehicle of their invasion. So Koons hints at a doom, which is linked to this gift that looks so promising from the outside. The sculpture's inner life, glaringly evoked by the coloured glaze transforms into the presence of death. This danger is not only directed against the ones who are given the present but also against the ones who give it. As we know, according to the myth the Roman Empire arose from Troy's decline, to conquer and colonise Greece. Giving and taking in the aesthetically armed capitalist society has a fatal core.[32]

Hence *Balloon Dog* fig. 18 is not just a monumental imitation and recognition of a childish balloon artwork. After a verbalisation of

31 'Peter-Klaus Schuster in Conversation' (note 25), p. 87. Also the following quotations.

32 At this point it also becomes clear that Koons referred to the polarisation of vital excess and the notion of vanitas in the earlier quoted statement on the oppositions of the age of Baroque.

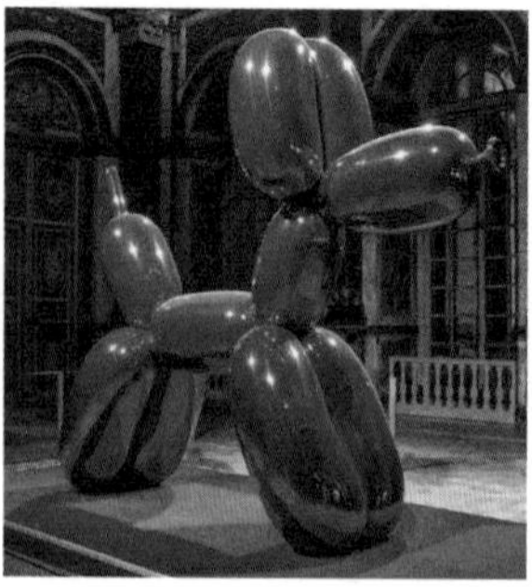

fig. 18

Jeff Koons,
Balloon Dog (Celebration),
1994–2000

Mirror-polished stainless steel with transparent colour coating, 307.3 x 363.2 x 114.3 cm. 5 unique versions (Blue, Magenta, Yellow, Orange, Red), photo: Jean-Pierre Dalbéra on Flickr

Hans Sedlmayr, it could be named a figuration of the empty centre,[33] a highly aggressive self-disempowerment of art, which is the only way for art to maintain its content of truth in a post-metaphysical era. This dialectical thought, however, was not supported by Sedlmayr but by Adorno, whom I connect with Koons at eye-level. The coloured glaze is another formation of the paradox of the empty volume, whose original form can be found in Koons' first real works of arts, the so-called *Inflatables*. The empty interior linked with outside gloss was also an artistic subject of vacuum cleaner works. Here and there Koons still strictly follows Marcel Duchamp's principle of the ready-made. He bought inflatable flowers and hares, putting them together with mirrored surfaces, which are normally used in salesrooms for the spectacular stagings of the goods: his first decisive artistic idea, out of which his whole œuvre is cogently developed.

Similar to the *Inflatables* from the *Celebration*-series, *Rabbit* is not a ready-made but a sculptural transformation, or, to be precise, a new creation of the ready-made, introduced by Duchamp himself[34] – a paradox constellation characterising the relation of the commodity as object and the autonomous work of art in the œuvre of Koons in general. With stainless steel an inflatable plastic animal is imitated, including all the crinkles and folds that occur at the seam when it is inflated. On account of the used material steel, which is utterly foreign to the object, *Rabbit* only remains the gestalt as a boundary of a manifold mirroring surface, which infinitely multiplies spectator and exhibition space – hence viciously making impossible an aesthetic experience. Koons exposes its merely narcissist function in the age of aesthetic capitalism. And yet due to its complex rejection of a classical evocative experience (anschauliche Erfahrung), *Rabbit* is great art and therefore addresses the senses as well as intellectual potentials.

In his quoted statement Koons defined the breath as the biological law of life. This becomes manifest in the interior of the *Inflatables* which, independent from their gestalt, are an alter ego

---

33 Hans Sedlmayr, *Verlust der Mitte: Die bildende Kunst des 19. und 20. Jahrhunderts als Symptom und Symbol der Zeit*, Salzburg, 1948. Isabelle Graw argued that Koons's leitmotif of the 'inner void' functions as a 'buffer to idealism'. Graw, 'There Is No Art in It' (note 14), p. 78.

34 See for instance Duchamp's *Paris Air* (1919) and *Beautiful Breath, Veil Water* (1921). Both objects also anticipate the issue of the empty volume that Koons deals with in his *Inflatables*.

of the human being and its vital energy. Is *Rabbit* then, just like *Balloon Dog* fig. 18, 'a metaphor for the excessive life, establishing the moment of inhalation as the expression of greatest vitality?'[35] Yes and no, since the breath is halted at the maximum of its extension – an image of the living within the image of death, unmistakably depicting the laws of the commodity as it has been analysed by Marx.[36] The vital work (*lebendige Arbeit*), objectified in the commodity, is only effective as deadened work insofar as the exchange value dominates the use value. Let me remind you here of the isolated diamond without a ring. This dominance of the exchange value is articulated by Koons in the shell character of his objects. Their emptiness is allegorised yet in a different manner by the mirroring surface as a reproductive superficiality. Koons himself has revolved around this ambiguous message of the material in somewhat dark phrases, which are significant for my interpretation: 'I also liked the fake luxury of stainless steel. It has always been the luxury of the proletariat. It was to seduce. The message was not to be seduced. Not to give up your economic power base. At the same time, anybody who bought one of these pieces would be giving in to his seduction. So it was enhancing my power.'[37]

Analogous to the metaphor of the Trojan horse, Koons talks about the fraud of the commodity, which betrays the consumer by the semblance of accessible wealth and alienates them from their own economic power. When Koons in the last sentence quoted here talks about his own power, the power of an artist, he appeals to the opposing reflexive semblance of art as a medium of truth, as I would argue. By means of a drastic character and the cool perfection of his production, Koons turns the semblance against itself.

The coldness of the mirroring surfaces cannot be humanised by the coloured gloss, which is introduced by Koons in *Celebration*. The abysmal, even monstrous, is actually strengthened by the monumental size of a gestalt which pretends to consist out of nothing more than air yet is formed massively like a classical sculpture. In contrast to *Rabbit*, the inflated volume of *Balloon*

---

35 Anette Hüsch, 'Archetypes for Survival: Or, How Art Can Comfort', in *Jeff Koons: Celebration* (note 25), pp. 97–110, here p. 108.

36 Duchamp hints at this meaning in his coffin-like ready-made *Beautiful Breath* (1921), mentioned above.

37 Jeff Koons – Anthony Haiden. Guest Interview, in: *Jeff Koons*, ed. Angelica Muthesius, Köln: Taschen, 1992, pp. 6-36, here p. 21.

Dog, about to burst, is increased by Koons, and so is the precarious balance between life and death. Within this antagonism of the effective forces, the force of the commodity clashes with the force of classical ancient art. Hence the philosopher Schelling praised the highest expression of life within the moment of death as the miracle of art on the example of the Niobe.[38] The crystalline, which Koons also forms in his *Diamond* series, was introduced by Schelling as a symbol of art, analogue to the beautiful indifference of antique sculpture. It visualises the simultaneity of vital growth and congealment.

The metaphor of the Trojan horse has demonstrated how Koons serves an allegory of art in the mask of the commodity fetish in *Celebration*. The gift, the jewellery and the children's toy as commodities are also symbols of art. Each of these three object spheres potentially leads towards the traditions of philosophical aesthetics. The theory of the gift, updated by Derrida after Mauss, is the most discussed figure of thought at the moment.[39] Yet, both jewellery and the play as frequently discussed origins of art have an anthropological signification which lays claim to art as a social practice being rooted in archaic rituals or techniques, beyond any bourgeois economics.

In context with the aesthetics of the play, a third anecdote concerning the genesis of the *Celebration* series is of importance. Koons mentions his little son whom he fathered with Illona Staller (Cicciolina) and whom he wants to prove his love to from the distance accrued by means of the sujet of the toy. The divorce from Staller was followed by an endless argument concerning the child's custody, the son was withdrawn from the father. Koons's dedication of the series to his beloved son is nevertheless a performative

---

38 Schellings Werke. After the original edition in new arrangement edited by Manfred Schröter. Dritter Ergänzungsband. *Zur Philosophie der Kunst 1803-1817*. C.H. Beck'sche Verlagsbuchhandlung München, 3. unveränderte Auflage 1985, p. 276. See also Regine Prange, 'Schellings Kristall: Zur Rezeptionsgeschichte einer Identitätsmetapher in Kunst und Kunsttheorie, mit Lacan betrachtet (Teil 1)', in *Imago: Internationales Jahrbuch für Psychoanalyse und Ästhetik*, Band 2, ed. Manfred Clemenz, Hans Zitko, Martin Büchsel and Diana Pflichthofer, Gießen, 2013, pp. 73–114, here p. 80.

39 Jacques Derrida, *Given Time: I. Counterfeit Money*, trans. Peggy Kamuf, Chicago, 1992. Derrida's point of reference is the short novel *La fausse monnaie* by Baudelaire, which generates the idea that art is like 'fausse monnaie', since art creates joy but is also business. Achim Hochdörfer discusses this dialectical thought in regard to Celebration. Hochdörfer, *The Gift of Art* (note 20).

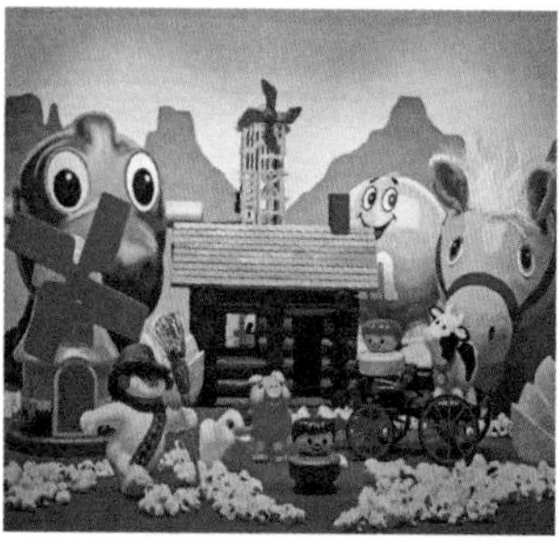

fig. 19

Jeff Koons,
Shelter (Celebration), 1996–1998
Oil on canvas, 300 x 376.2 cm,
photo: Fred Romero on FLickr

statement, since the children's toy has been a preferred subject of Koons's long before his short marriage with Cicciolina. What he demonstrates with his story, is the general pervasion of the most personal, tender feelings with the attraction of the commodity.

As the *Celebration* series made clear, Koons uses his own personality, his love life and family life in order to impart theatrical reality to the functioning of the commodity aesthetics. Its exaggeration, of course, leads to the analytical thought, towards a criticism, which can be placed next to Wolfgang Fritz Haug's critique of commodity aesthetics.[40] Within the child as recipient of the toy product, Koons also demonstrates the historical dimension of exchange, which is directed towards the future: children are the ones receiving the fatal gift of the Trojan horse. They are Trojans, who, as children who are playing and living with vitality, receive a gift which teaches them to link their desire to the gestalt of the commodity. Hence they are depraved, even before they, themselves, as grown up wage workers solidify into the commodity of the labour force (*Arbeitskraft*). The promise of emancipation, one's own life and creativity – a general theme connected to the aestheticisation of the commodity, derived by Koons from Warhol's *Do It Yourself* series, has already been talked about here. In the interview, Koons associates the joy in the material with this: 'I always enjoyed material when it is just revealing itself.'[41] What is this 'true face' of steel and plastic in reference to the promise of an intense life?

The mythological moment inherent to the plastic material was already defined by Roland Barthes in his *Mythologies* of everyday life as an evocation of a seemingly indefinite metamorphosic force of transformation.[42] Everything can be made out of plastic. Plates and dishes, even the human heart can be reproduced out of plastic. As a material it thus represents the sense of a second nature replacing the first one. Koons also hints at this direction when he explains his allegiance to polyethylene: 'It is a material that gives children an adult fantasy for the first time. Polyethylene is used a lot to make toys for children; their own play house in the backyard.'[43]

---

40 See note 7.

41 'Peter-Klaus Schuster in Conversation' (note 25), p. 87.

42 Roland Barthes, 'Plastic', in *Mythologies* (1957), selected and translated from the French by Annette Lavers, New York, 1991, pp. 97–9.

43 'Peter-Klaus Schuster in Conversation' (note 25), p. 87.

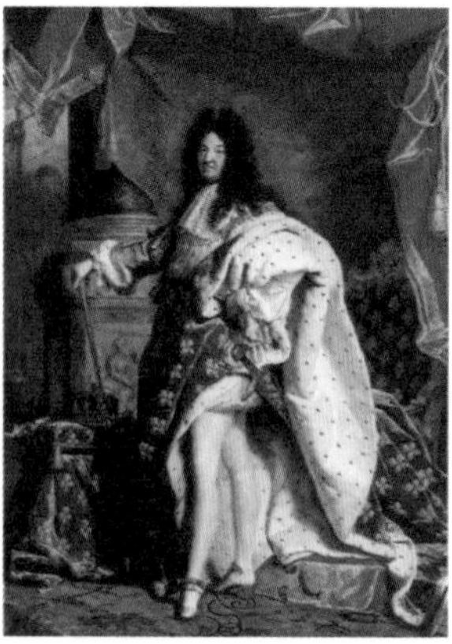

fig. 20

Hyazinthe Rigaud,
Portrait de Louis XIV, 1701
Oil on canvas, 277 x 184 cm

*Shelter*fig. 19 shows such a world of toys made out of plastic together with pieces of popcorn – a children's paradise, the gloss of which is contradicted by a likewise drastic and sign-like simplified expression of the playing figures. An advertising image would look different. With the aid of the Surrealist shift of proportions,[44] Koons transforms the children's room's cute symbiosis of animal and human, which we already know from *Banality*, into an expression of the uncanny, and hence into the sense of a depersonalisation. Imagining oneself to be a grown up – and this condition continues in Koons's world also throughout adulthood – actually means the lust for self-estrangement. The polyethylene, just like the quasi-sacral gloss of the steel, is directed towards a negation of a rational instance of the self. Celebration hence means the permanence of the infantile suspension of the self, which sustainably dissolves the art-immanent sphere of the play, which is also referred to here. Yet the play, which Schiller once claimed was a supposed counterpart to the asocial semblance of art,[45] cannot be separated from the treacherous aesthetic semblance, despite its 'innocent aura', as Koons demonstrates.

It is not the promise of a childlike vital space to live but the breaking of this promise, demonstrated by the artistic arrangement, which transports – in line with Adorno – truth, namely the request to reappropriate the reified wealth.

Koons at Versailles: Moon

This last chapter should again clarify how Koons has his material speak and argue. Our point of reference is the exhibition at Versailles in 2008, which admits particular significance to the *Celebration* series and unfolds a historical discourse by the arrangement of the objects. In the following I will focus on the nature motives in Koons's objects, which we already observed in the *Diamond* works, in the subject of the egg and also in the communities of animals, humans and plants.

---

44 See René Magritte's interiors with enlarged objects, e.g. *La Géante* (1929) or *Les valeurs personelles* (1952).

45 Friedrich Schiller, 'Über die ästhetische Erziehung des Menschen in einer Reihe von Briefen', in *Schillers Werke*, vol. 4: *Schriften*, Frankfurt am Main, 1966, pp. 193–286, here p. 238: 'der Mensch spielt nur, wo er in voller Bedeutung des Worts Mensch ist, und er ist nur da ganz Mensch, wo er spielt.'

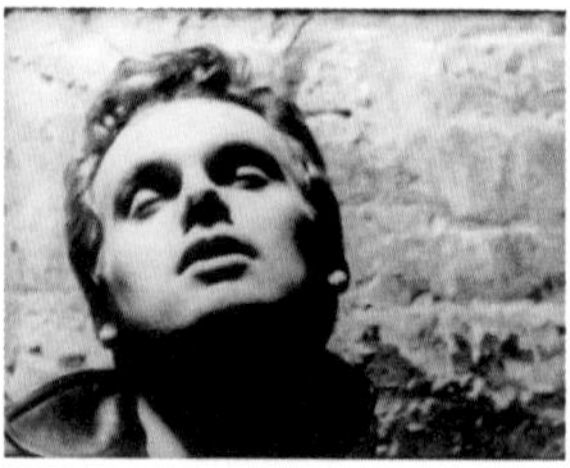

fig. 21

Andy Warhol,
Blow Job, 1964
36 minutes film, 16 mm,
Actor: DeVeren Bookwalter

The fact that this imagery of nature and its inherent non-human potential of infinite transformative capacity actually discusses the instruments of power, is obvious within the art world of the Sun King. Koons stages two of his works as particularly programmatic answers to the absolute sovereignty of the monarch.

The *Self Portrait* in marble from the series *Made in Heaven* is placed opposite the official portrait of Louis XIV [fig. 20]. The artist is naked, a blissful smile on his face, the eyes are closed. His swelling bust hovers over crystals, as if he had materialised out of this non-organic sphere. The art-theoretical thought cannot be missed due to the spatial relation to the king in his ermine: the bourgeois artist provokes and yet has taken up the succession of the absolute sovereign. He, as well, legitimises himself through the authority of nature, Louis XIV quoted by means of the ermine and also with his reference to the sun and the Greek god Apollon, who was adored as Helios in antiquity.[46] Yet Koons calls upon neither the sun nor Apollon, nor the vital animal ornament of the ermine. His empire is the night, the unconscious, irrational. Whereas the Baroque emperor demonstrates his transcendent persona in the painting with an enormous robe, a wig and the insignia of his power, the bourgeois artist reclaims himself as absolute nature. In a sarcastic manner Koons develops his artist persona out of a pose with Cicciolina, which, by the way, hints at an orgiastic climax, again the transcendence of absent-mindedness (*Selbstvergessenheit*). The motive and its fragmented representation reminds us of Andy Warhol's film *Blow Job* [fig. 21] which is likewise designed as a portrait. Just like Warhol negates the films grammar by rejecting the reverse shot, thus not showing the source of the lust which is mirrored on the protagonist's face, Koons negates the logic of the sculptural genre, which also claims narrative context. Hence it would be a misunderstanding to think that Koons represents himself in his *Self-Portrait* like the king in his portrait is represented. Koons's autonomy is not a personal one it is the aesthetic autonomy of the montage. Only by means of this intellectual force can Koons be grasped as an artist. A multitude of art-historical references enters this montage and reveals the sense of this lack of subjectivity (*Subjektlosigkeit*), which the artist

46 Many sculptures and paintings at Versailles represent Apollon as the alter ego of the Sun King Louis XIV, (https://andrelenotre.com/apollon-mythe-et-representation-dans-les-jardins-de-versailles/, accessed 9 June 2018).

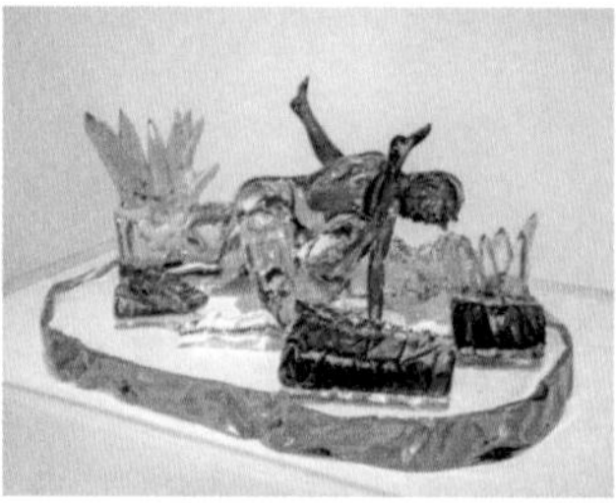

fig. 22

Jeff Koons,
Violet - Ice (Kama Sutra),
Made in Heaven, 1991
Glass, 33 x 71.1 x 43.2 cm,
photo: Fred Romero on Flickr

personally does not at all worship. He rather uses this paradigm as a role model of his artistry and reflects upon it.

It is obviously the Romantic genius, inspired by love and the unconscious, which Koons stages in his own persona. Sarcastically he connects this allegory of the Romantic genius with the neo-Classicist form of the marble bust, thus revealing the contrast between the Romantic trust in the forces of the irrational and the still maintained humanist idea of the heroic individual. Within the motive of the crystal, Koons refers, as mentioned above, to a metaphor of art initiated by Schelling, which can be observed in the aesthetic production of modernity up until today. In Koons's œuvre we encountered it in Diamond, and the crystalline also accompanied or even embodied the theatre of sexual ecstasy in the series Made in Heaven fig. 22. By means of the process of montage, Koons compresses two symbols which support the modern concept of art, proving its objectivity beyond any subjective capriciousness: the crystal as nature's form of art and the psychic energy which can be increased towards ecstasy. Both those symbols are, by the way, also part of the neo-Romantic, Surrealist repertoire of images, which Koons also likes to use. Reproduced in 1934 in the review *Minotaure*, a photography of crystals by Brassaï illustrates Breton's concept of 'convulsive beauty', meaning life (in his energetic substance) as art.[47] Salvador Dali's photo-montage *The Phenomenon of Ecstasy* (1933) demonstrates the analogy of erotic and religious abandon of the self, which Koons also thematises in Made in Heaven. His critical impact consists in making visible the conformism of the Surrealist homage to the irrational, not least by the translation of Surrealist aesthetics into a kitschy opulence of material, which always refers to the industrial apparatus of exploitation. In other words: capitalism is identified as the actual non-human power, which the surrealists worshipped as the non-bourgeois principle of life. Koons recognises the crystal as the absolute figuration of the gloss, the material of an ideal, which has left behind any social and rational conditionality and thus finds its projection surface in the loving embrace.

Now we have reached the paradox of the crystalline *kamasutra* positions fig. 22, which mark Koons as a canny analyst of sexual revolution. However, the white marble of his Self-Portrait, in itself a crystalline rock, mediates connotations, has its own face. By means of

47 André Breton, 'La beauté sera convulsive', in *Minotaure* 5 (1934), pp. 9–10, 12–14, here p. 9. See Prange, '*Schellings Kristall*' (note 38), p. 104, ill. 5.

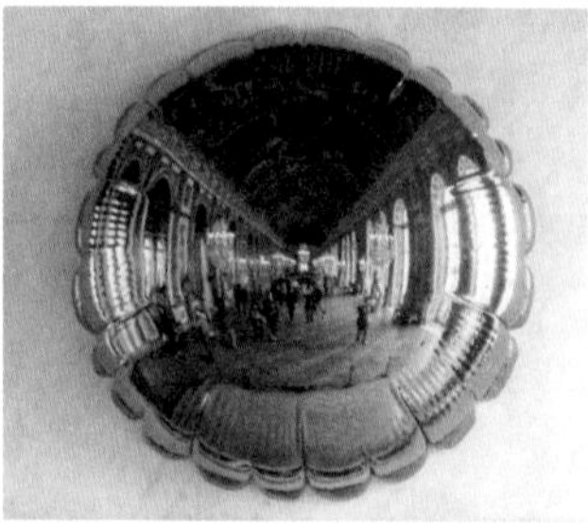

fig. 23

Jeff Koons,
Moon (Celebration),
1995–2000

Mirror-polished stainless steel with transparent colour coating, 315 x 315 x 101.6 cm, 5 unique versions (Light Blue, Light Pink, Silver, Violet, Yellow), photo: Achim Hepp on Flickr this material, Koons reached for Gian Lorenzo Bernini's *Saint Teresa* (1645–52), hit by Amor's arrow. Furthermore Teresa might be understood as the prototype alter ego of the ecstatic artist, especially since Koons also signals a floating of his rudimentary gestalt, a floating, by the way, which establishes contact to the Inflatables, the balloon sculptures. They are all, as incarnations of the gloss, images of the artist and of his realm of semblance.

At Versailles the golden gloss of the stucco ornaments, candelabra, frames of paintings and mirrors were competing with the fake steel gloss of Koons's sculptures. This disharmonious competition underlines in the castle's spatial context the neo-feudal but also religious character of aesthetic capitalism, which art cannot just abandon but has to historically reclaim by means of self-criticism.

Finally, let's have a look at *Moon (Light Blue)* fig. 23, a work of the *Celebration* series, within which, as well, a clear answer to the Sun King and his claim to power is formulated, particularly since as a mirror object, it was placed in the world-famous hall of mirrors. In this room, Koons found the historical role model of the department store mirrors which he used for his first Inflatables. It is perhaps worth to note that he, in his own words, got to know Versailles through the buildings of the Bavarian King Ludwig II.[48] Hence he thematises the castle in its trivial-artistic, touristic appropriation, as a construct which relinquished its political significance to aesthetic functions.

The work *Moon* is mysterious, even though its figural role model, a bottle cap, remains clearly visible. It is not just the monumental format which creates this alienation. The high-gloss surface transforms it into a mirror on the wall, which joins all the other mirrors in the galerie des Glaces. Its coloration, on the other hand, withdraws something of this mirror function and transforms the object into a picture. Its title, *Moon*, transforms the figural form of use of the bottle cap into the image of a star. The fact that it is the nocturnal star and not the sun, complements the iconography of the self-portrait, mobilising the poetic power of the dark world of the libidinal urge against the Sun King.

I would like to introduce another reference, which leads us back to the beginning of this essay. I think that Koons's *Moon* is another paraphrase of the Arnolfini Wedding fig. 3. Koons isolated

48 'I knew Versailles through photos and through other readaptions of Versailles such as Ludwig II's in Bavaria.' 'Jeff Koons by Michel Houellebecq', in Jean-Jacques Aillagon (ed.), *Jeff Koons Versailles*, Paris, 2008, pp. 15–21, here p. 21.

the self-referential motive of the mirror and revealed its symbolic meaning as a symbol of painting. The mirror gains autonomy by becoming the gestalt of the picture itself. Jan van Eyck's relief of the frame with its small miniatures of scenes of Christ's Passion, the contemplative use of which is illustrated by the rosary hanging next to the mirror, is replaced by Koons with the curly edges of the bottle cap, which refers to an utterly different use: the consumption of industrial products, for instance a Coca Cola bottle. Again, Warhol seems to be Koons's dialogue partner, since he praised Coca Cola as a democratic blessing, a luxury accessible to each and everyone, from the president to the petit-bourgeois and even the beggar.[49] Koons unfolds Warhol's heritage by, among other things, combining consumers' pleasures with religious salvation as anticipated in the latter's already commented *Golden Marilyn* fig. 10 and his late paintings *Raphael I - $ 6.99* (1985) and *The Last Supper* (1986).[50] Due to the enchanting gloss of the blue *Moon*, the consumption of commodities is, moreover, interpreted as a kind of confusing gaze into the crystal (*Kristallschau*), which replaces religious contemplation, adding the reference to magical power.

As described at the beginning, the historical shift from inner, religious practice to a glorification of everyday things has already been prepared by means of the innovative techniques of pictorial realism, established by oil paint and perspective construction. The fact that Koons places particular emphasis on the continuation of oil painting's technique proves him to be a conscious recipient of the complete early modern tradition, which, however, he unfailingly

---

49 According to Warhol American consumerism realised an equality of thought that Bertolt Brecht and the Soviet Union had intended to reach via Communism. The structuralist wit in Warhol's remarks reveals the critical power of his art: 'All the Cokes are the same and all the Cokes are good. Liz Taylor knows it, the President knows it, the bum knows it, and you know it. [...] Russia is doing it under government. It's happening here all by itself without being under a strict government; so if it's working without trying, why can't it work without being Communist? Everybody looks alike and acts alike, and we're getting more and more that way.' G. R. Svenson, 'What is Pop Art? Answers from 8 Painters', Part I, *Artnews* 62, November 1963, p. 26, quoted from 'Warhol in His Own Words', in Kynaston McShine (ed.), *Andy Warhol Retrospective*, exh. cat. Museum of Modern Art, New York, 1989, pp. 457–67, here p. 458. Ironically in Warhol's paintings of Coca Cola Bottles, a cap is missing! If we understand Koons's *Moon* as a critical response to Warhol, it is again the reality and function of the product he emphasises and analyses, whereas Warhol appropriates the product in an aestheticised mode.

50 Ibid., pp. 390-391, cat. nos 453-454.

breaks by means of the method of montage. Van Eyck's mirror no longer shows an interior picture in Koons's *Moon*, but rather mirrors the space in front, like an ordinary mirror. The quote of van Eyck transforms this into a philosophical reflection: we, standing in front of the *Moon* mirror object, are inside the picture, part of the picture. We cannot reach an outside, since our social existence is trapped within the images of aesthetic capitalism. The resulting lack of historical consciousness is crossed by Koons with his quotes and restagings of sacral, magical and feudal gloss, predecessors of aesthetic semblance.

On the authors

Wilhelm Lindemann is a freelance curator and writer. He has worked as a curator and manager of festivals and cultural events for many years. Between 2001 and 2018 Lindemann headed the project of restoring and converting the Jakob Bengel Factory, a historic industrial building in Idar-Oberstein, to a cultural monument and museum. Since 2005 he has curated Thinking Jewellery, the academic colloquium at the Trier University of Applied Sciences, Campus Idar-Oberstein, and a wide range of jewellery exhibitions.

Olaf Müller studied mathematics and philosophy in Göttingen; since 2003 he is Professor of Natural Philosophy at the Humboldt University in Berlin. In his writings, he deals with the epistemological question of whether we could always be connected to a deceptively real computer simulation (answer: no, see www.GehirnImTank.de), with moral problems of climate change and humanitarian war interventions, and with the puzzle of what bodiless survival after death might look like. In his 2015 book "Mehr Licht" he defended Goethe's theory of colours (Fischer, 2015; www.farbenstreit.de).

Regine Prange studied art history, classical archaeology, modern history and sociology in Munich and Berlin; 1991 doctorate at the FU Berlin; 1998 habilitation. Since 2001 Chair of Modern and Contemporary Art History, Art and Media Theory at the Goethe University of Frankfurt am Main. Her main areas of research are: History of abstract painting; utopias and theories of modernity; history of art history and its methods; the aesthetic construction of space in painting and film.

Imprint

 photo credits Despite every effort to do so, not all copyright holders could be identified due to the 2020 Covid 19 pandemic. If you are a copyright holder and were not contacted, please write to art@arnoldsche.com www.arnoldsche.com editors Wilhelm Lindemann, Theo Smeets authors Wilhelm Lindemann, Olaf Müller, Regine Prange translations John Maddox, Valérie Wagner, Katrin Kolk copy editors Wendy Brouwer, Oranna Kammann graphic design Cornelia Wruck, Theo Smeets cover design Karina Moschke arnoldsche project manager Matthias Becher printed by DZS Grafik d.o.o., Ljubljana, on 120 g/m² Munken Pure bibliographic information published by the Deutsche Nationalbibliothek. The Deutsche Nationalbibliothek lists this publication in the Deutsche Nationalbibliografie; detailed bibliographic data are available at www.dnb.de ISBN 978-3-89790-539-9 made in Europe, 2020